海军工程大学涉外丛书

外训系列教材

Warship Electronic Technology Basics

舰艇电子技术基础

主　编　朱旭芳　钟　斌
副主编　马知远　潘　丽　吴文全　范　越

武汉大学出版社

图书在版编目(CIP)数据

舰艇电子技术基础/朱旭芳,钟斌主编.—武汉:武汉大学出版社,2017.4(2023.2 重印)
海军工程大学涉外丛书
ISBN 978-7-307-18882-2

Ⅰ.舰… Ⅱ.①朱… ②钟… Ⅲ.军用船—模拟电路—电路分析—高等学校—教材 Ⅳ.①U674.7 ②TN710

中国版本图书馆 CIP 数据核字(2016)第 288737 号

责任编辑:胡 艳　　责任校对:汪欣怡　　版式设计:马 佳

出版发行:武汉大学出版社　　(430072　武昌　珞珈山)
(电子邮箱:cbs22@whu.edu.cn　网址:www.wdp.com.cn)
印刷:武汉邮科印务有限公司
开本:720×1000　1/16　印张:15　字数:352 千字　插页:1
版次:2017 年 4 月第 1 版　　2023 年 2 月第 2 次印刷
ISBN 978-7-307-18882-2　　定价:30.00 元

版权所有,不得翻印;凡购我社的图书,如有质量问题,请与当地图书销售部门联系调换。

前　言

"海军工程大学涉外丛书"所属的外训系列教材是外国留学生来校学习培训的专用教材，也可作为中国军校学员专业英语培训及双语教学的辅助教材。该系列教材的逐步推出和完善，是海军工程大学对外军事教育在教学理念、教学模式和条件建设上不断努力与探索的结果，必将更好地满足外国留学生的教学需求。其主要特点是：

1. 遵循海军工程大学《外训人才培养方案》和《外训课程标准》，以结构、功能、文化相结合为原则，以提高外国留学生的军事职业素养和专业综合技能为目标。

2. 内容的选择，强调突出各专业、各课程的知识体系及发展前沿，贴近外国军队建设和装备实际，并根据时代特点和外国留学生实际情况进行调整和补充，注重题材的丰富性和体裁的多样化。

3. 教材公开出版前，均邀请校内外的专家同行及外国留学生审阅、修改，并在多年的外训教学实践中进行锤炼和检验。

《舰艇电子技术基础》是"海军工程大学涉外丛书——外训系列教材"之一。全书共分十二章，系统而简要地介绍模拟和数字电子技术的基本组成、基本原理和基本分析设计方法。是一本有关舰艇和现代电子技术的基础读物。可以使学生了解电子技术的发展历史和现状，掌握电子技术的基本知识，开阔技术视野，培养职业素养，奠定下一步专业学习的基础。

本书由朱旭芳、钟斌负责纲目拟定和全书编写统稿，潘丽负责全书的文稿校对、插图和数字部分的编写工作，朱旭芳、马知远、吴文全负责模拟部分编写工作，范越负责习题和参考答案的编写工作。编写过程中，参考了大量国内外文献，吸收了国内外学者的最新研究成果。海军工程大学龚梅副教授为本书的英文审校付出了大量心血。武汉大学出版社为本书的出版提供了有力帮助。在此向各位专家、学者表示衷心的感谢。由于作者水平有限，书中难免存在疏漏和不当之处，敬请专家和读者提出宝贵意见。

编　者

2016 年 12 月

目 录

Introduction ··· 1

Chapter 1　Diodes and Applications ································ 7
   1.1　Introduction ··· 7
   1.2　Ideal Diodes ··· 7
   1.3　Practical Diodes ·· 8
   1.4　Physical Operation of Junction Diodes ···················· 9
       1.4.1　Diode Junction ·· 9
       1.4.2　Forward-Biased Condition ···························· 12
       1.4.3　Reverse-Biased Condition ···························· 12
       1.4.4　Breakdown Condition ·································· 13
   1.5　Characteristics of Practical Diodes ·························· 14
       1.5.1　Forward-Biased Region ······························· 16
       1.5.2　Reverse-Biased Region ······························· 16
       1.5.3　Breakdown Region ···································· 16
   1.6　Zener Diodes ·· 17
   1.7　Light-Emitting Diodes ·· 19
   1.8　Applications of Diodes ··· 19
       1.8.1　Diode Rectifiers ·· 20
       1.8.2　Clippers ·· 24
       1.8.3　Output Filters for Rectifiers ························· 27

Chapter 2　Amplifiers ·· 35
   2.1　Bipolar Junction Transistor ····································· 36

  2.1.1 Principle ·· 37
  2.1.2 Input and Output Characteristics ······································ 38
 2.2 Low-frequency Amplifiers ·· 40
  2.2.1 DC Biasing Circuits ··· 40
  2.2.2 Analyzing Methods of Amplifiers ····································· 43
  2.2.3 Common-Emitters ··· 47
  2.2.4 Emitter Followers ·· 50
 2.3 Field-Effect Transistors ··· 52
 2.4 Cascaded Amplifiers ·· 54
  2.4.1 Input Resistance ·· 55
  2.4.2 Output Resistance ·· 56
  2.4.3 Voltage Gain of the Multi-stage Amplifier ·························· 57
  2.4.4 Frequency Response of the RC-coupled Amplifier ················· 58
 2.5 Active Sources and Differential Amplifiers ································· 59
  2.5.1 Internal Structure of Differential Amplifiers ······················· 59
  2.5.2 BJT Current Sources ··· 61
  2.5.3 Characteristics of Differential Amplifiers ·························· 66
  2.5.4 Differential Amplifier Circuit ·· 68
 2.6 Power Amplifiers ·· 76
  2.6.1 Classification of Power Amplifiers ·································· 77
  2.6.2 Class B Complementary Push-pull Amplifiers ····················· 79
  2.6.3 Complementary Class AB Push-Pull Amplifiers ··················· 81

Chapter 3 Feedback Amplifiers ·· 91
 3.1 The Basic Concept of Feedback Amplifiers ································ 91
 3.2 The Principle of Negative Feedback ··· 92
 3.3 Feedback Topologies ··· 93
 3.4 Identifying the Type of Negative Feedback Amplifier ···················· 96
 3.5 Approximate Calculation of A_f ··· 98

Chapter 4 Oscillators ·· 102
 4.1 Principles of Oscillators ··· 102

      4.1.1 Frequency Stability ·· 104
      4.1.2 Amplitude Stability ·· 104
  4.2 Phase-Shift Oscillators ··· 105
  4.3 Wien-Bridge Oscillators ·· 108
  4.4 Colpitts Oscillators ·· 111
  4.5 Hartley Oscillators ·· 115
  4.6 Crystal Oscillators ··· 118

Chapter 5 Operational Amplifiers 122
  5.1 Characteristics of Ideal Op-Amps ····································· 122
  5.2 Analysis of Circuits with Ideal Op-Amp ···························· 125
      5.2.1 Inverting Amplifier ·· 125
      5.2.2 Noninverting Amplifier ·· 126
      5.2.3 Differential Amplifier ··· 127
  5.3 Applications ··· 128
      5.3.1 The Integrator ·· 128
      5.3.2 The Differentiator ··· 129
      5.3.3 Noninverting Summing Amplifier ···························· 130
      5.3.4 Inverting Summing Amplifier ································· 131
      5.3.5 Addition-Subtraction Amplifier ······························· 132
  5.4 Active Filters ·· 133
      5.4.1 Low-Pass Filter ·· 133
      5.4.2 High-pass Active Filter ·· 135
      5.4.3 Bandpass Filter ·· 135
  5.5 Comparator ··· 136
      5.5.1 Basic Inverting Schmitt Trigger ······························ 139
      5.5.2 Voltage Transfer Characteristic ······························· 139

Chapter 6 Introductory Digital Concepts 147
  6.1 Digital and Analog Quantities ··· 147
  6.2 Binary Digitals, Logic Levels and Digital Waveforms ·········· 147
      6.2.1 Binary Digits ··· 147

6.2.2 Logic Levels 148
6.2.3 Digital Waveforms 148
6.2.4 The Pulse 149

Chapter 7 Number Systems, Operations, and Codes 153
7.1 Binary-to-Decimal Conversion 153
7.2 Decimal-to-Binary Conversion 153
7.3 Binary Addition 155

Chapter 8 Logic Gates 158
8.1 The Basic Logic Gates 158
8.2 Fixed-Function Logic 159

Chapter 9 Boolean Switching Algebra 162
9.1 Boolean Operations and Expressions 162
9.2 Laws and Rules of Boolean Algebra 163
    9.2.1 Laws of Boolean Algebra 163
    9.2.2 Rules of Boolean Algebra 164
9.3 DeMorgan's Theorems 164
9.4 Simplification Using Boolean Algebra 165
9.5 Boolean Expressions and Truth Tables 167
    9.5.1 The Sum-of-Products (SOP) Form 167
    9.5.2 The Product-of-Sums (POS) Form 167
    9.5.3 The truth table 168
9.6 The Karnaugh Map 169

Chapter 10 Combinational Logic 173
10.1 Definition of Combinational Logic 173
10.2 Functions of Combinational Logic 175
    10.2.1 Adders 175
    10.2.2 Encoders 176
    10.2.3 Multiplexers 181

Chapter 11　Latches, Flip-Flops and Timers ········ 186

　11.1　Latches ················· 186

　　　11.1.1　The S-R (Set-Reset) Latch ············ 186

　11.2　Flip-Flops ················ 187

　　　11.2.1　The Edge-Triggered S-R Flip-Flop ········ 187

　　　11.2.2　The Edge-Triggered D Flip-Flop ········· 188

　　　11.2.3　The Edge-Triggered J-K Flip-Flop ········ 188

　　　11.2.4　Flip-Flop Applications ············· 189

　11.3　One-shots ················ 191

　11.4　The Astable Multivibrator ············ 194

Chapter 12　Counters and Shift Registers ············· 199

　12.1　Counters ················· 199

　　　12.1.1　Asynchronous Counters ············ 199

　　　12.1.2　Synchronous Counters ············ 200

　12.2　Shift Registers ··············· 202

Appendix A　Testing Solid-state Components ·········· 207

Appendix B　Answers to All the Problems ············ 210

Introduction

We encounter electronics in our daily life in the form of telephones, radios, televisions, audio equipment, home appliances, computers and equipment for industrial control and automation. Electronics have become the stimuli for and an integral part of modern technological growth and development. The field of electronics deals with the design and applications of electronic devices.

History of Electronics

The age of electronics began with the invention of the first amplifying device, the triode vacuum tube, by Fleming in 1904. This invention was followed by the development of the solid-state point-contact diode (silicon) by Pickard in 1906, the first radio circuits from diodes and triodes between 1907 and 1927, the superheterodyne receiver by Armstrong in 1920, demonstration of television in 1925, and the field-effect device by Lilienfield in 1925, fm modulation by Armstrong in 1933, and radar in 1940.

The first electronics revolution began in 1947 with the invention of the silicon transistor by Bardeen, Bratain and Shockley at Bell Laboratories. Most of today's advanced electronic technologies are traceable to that invention, as modem microelectronics evolved over the years from the semiconductors. This revolution was followed by the first demonstration of color television in 1950 and the invention of the unipolar field effect transistor by Shockley in 1952.

The next breakthrough came in 1956, when Bell Laboratories developed the pnpn triggering transistor, also known as a thyristor or a silicon-controlled rectifier (SCR). The second electronics revolution began with the development of a commercial thyristor by General Electric Company in 1958. That was the beginning of a new era for applications of electronics in power processing or conditioning, called power electronics. Since then, many different types of power semiconductor devices and conversion techniques have been developed. The first integrated circuit (IC) was developed in 1958 simultaneously by Kilby at Texas Instruments and Noyce & Moore at Fairchild Semiconductor, marking the beginning of a new phase in the microelectronics revolution. This invention was followed by development of the first commercial IC operational amplifier, the μA709, by Fairchild Semiconductor in 1968; the 4004 microprocessor by Intel in 1971; the 8-bit microprocessor by Intel in 1972; and the gigabit memory chip by Intel in 1995. IC development continues today, in an effort to achieve higher density chips with lower power dissipation; historical levels of in integration in circuits are shown in Table 1.

Table 1

DATE	Degree of Integration	Number of Component per chip
1950s	Discrete components	1 to 2
1960s	Small-scale integration (SSI)	Fewer then 10^2
1966	Medium-scale integration (MSI)	From 10^2 to 10^3
1969	Large-scale integration (LSI)	From 10^3 to 10^4
1975	Very-large-scale integration (VLSI)	From 10^4 to 10^9
1990s	Ultra-large-scale integration (ULSI)	More than 10^9

Electronic Systems

An electronic system is an arrangement of electronic devices and components with a defined set of inputs and outputs. Using transistors (trans-resistors) as devices, it takes in information in the form of input signals (or simply inputs), performs operations on them, and then produces output signals (or outputs). Electronic systems may be categorized according to the type of application, such as communication system, medical electronics, instrumentation, control system, or computer system.

A block diagram of an fm radio receiver is shown in Figure 1 (a). The antenna acts the sensor. The input signal from the antenna is small, usually in the μV range; its amplitude and power level are then amplified by the electronic system before the signal is fed into the speaker. A block diagram of a temperature display instrument is shown in Figure 1 (b). The output drives the display instrument. The temperature sensor produces a small voltage, usually in millivolts per unit temperature rise above 0 degrees celsius (e.g., 1 mV/℃). Both systems take an input from a sensor, process it, and produce an output to drive an actuator.

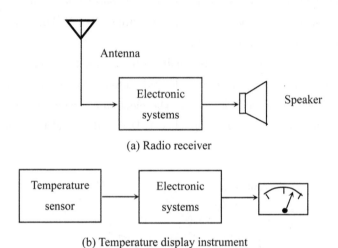

(a) Radio receiver

(b) Temperature display instrument

Figure 1 Electronic Systems

An electronic system must communicate with input and output devices. In general, the inputs and outputs are in the form of electrical signals. The input signals may be derived from the measurement of physical qualities such as temperature or liquid level, and the outputs may be used to vary other physical qualities such as those displays and heating elements. Electronic systems often use sensors to sense external input qualities and actuators to control external output qualities. Sensors and actuators are often called transducers. The loudspeaker is an example of a transducer that converts an electronic signal into sound.

Electronic Signals and Notation

Electronic signals can be separated into two categories: analog and digital. An analog signal has a continuous range of amplitudes over time, as shown in Figure 2(a). A digital signal assumes only discrete voltage values over time, as shown in Figure 2(b). A digital signal has only two values, representing binary logic state 1 (for high level) and binary logic state 0 (for low level). In order to accommodate variations in component values, temperature, and noise (or extraneous signals), logic sate 1 is usually assigned to any voltage between 2~5 V. Logic state 0 may be assigned to any voltage between 0~0.8 V.

The output signal of a sensor is usually of the analog type, and actuators often require analog input to produce the desired output. An analog signal can be converted to digital form and vice versa. The electronic circuits that perform these conversions are called analog-to-digital (A/D) and digital-to-analog (D/A) converters.

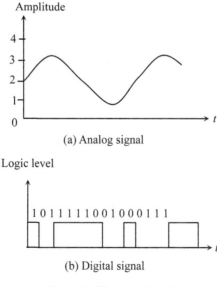

(a) Analog signal

(b) Digital signal

Figure 2 Electronic Signals

An analog signal is normally represented by a symbol with a subscript. The symbol and the subscript can be either uppercase or lowercase, according to the conventions shown in Table 2. For example, consider the circuit in Figure 3 (a), whose input consists of a dc voltage $V_{DC}=5$ V and an ac voltage $v_{ac}=2\sin\omega t$. The instantaneous voltages are shown in Figure 3 (b). The definitions of voltage and current symbols are as follows:

(1) V_{DC}, I_{DC} are dc values: uppercase variables and uppercase subscripts.

$$V_{DC}=5\text{V}$$
$$I_{DC}=\frac{V_{DC}}{R_L}=5\text{ mA}$$

(2) v_{ab}, i_a are instantaneous ac values: lowercase variables and lowercase subscripts.

$$v_{ab}=v_{ac}=2\sin\omega t$$
$$i_a=2\sin\omega t\text{ mA}\quad(\text{for }R_L=1\text{ k}\Omega)$$

(3) v_{AB}, i_A are total instantaneous values: lowercase variables and uppercase sub-scripts.

$$v_{AB}=V_{DC}+v_{ab}=5+2\sin\omega t$$
$$i_A=I_{DC}+i_a=5\text{ mA}+2\sin\omega t\text{ mA}\quad(\text{for }R_L=1\text{ k}\Omega)$$

(4) V_{ab}, I_a are total magnitude values: upper variables and lowercase subscripts.

$$V_{ab}=\sqrt{5^2+(\sqrt{2})^2}=5.2\text{V}$$
$$I_a=\sqrt{5^2+(\sqrt{2})^2}=5.2\text{mA}$$

Table 2

Definition	Quantity	Subscript	Example
dc value of the signal	Uppercase	Uppercase	V_D
ac value of the signal	Lowercase	Lowercase	v_d
Total instantaneous value of the signal (dc and ac)	Lowercase	Uppercase	v_D
Complex variable, phasor, or rms value of the signal	Uppercase	Lowercase	V_d

6 — Introduction

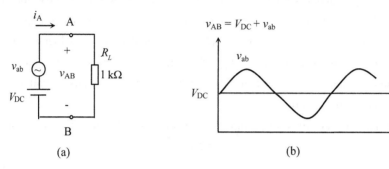

Figure 3　Notation for Electronic Signals

Chapter 1

Diodes and Applications

1.1 Introduction

A diode is a two-terminal semiconductor device. It offers a low resistance on the order of mΩ in one direction and a high resistance on the order of GΩ in the other direction. Thus a diode permits an easy current flow in only one direction. The diode is a simplest electronic device, and a basic building block for many electronic circuits and systems. In this chapter, we will discuss the characteristics of diodes.

The diode exhibits a nonlinear relation between the voltage across its terminals and the current through it. However, the analysis of the diode can be greatly simplified with the assumption of an ideal characteristic. The results of this simplified analysis are useful in understanding the operation of diode circuits and are acceptable in many practical cases, especially at the initial stage of design and analysis. If more accurate results are required, linear circuit models representing the nonlinear characteristic of diodes can be used. These models are commonly used in evaluating the performance of diode circuits. If better accuracy is required, however, computer-aided modeling and simulation are normally used.

1.2 Ideal Diodes

The symbol for a semiconductor diode is shown in Figure 1.2.1(a). Its two terminals are the anode and the cathode, respectively. If the anode voltage is held positive with respect to the cathode terminal, the diode conducts and offers a small forward resistance. The diode is then said to be forward biased, and it behaves as a short circuit, as shown in Figure 1.2.1(b). If the anode voltage is kept negative with respect to the cathode terminal, the diode offers a high resistance. The diode is then said to be reverse biased and it behaves as an open circuit, as shown in Figure 1.2.1(c). Thus an ideal diode will offer zero resistance and zero voltage drop in the forward direction. In the reverse direction, it will offer infinite resistance and allow zero current.

An ideal diode acts as a short circuit in the forward region of conduction ($v_D = 0$) and as an open circuit in the reverse region of conduction ($i_D = 0$). The v-i characteristic of an ideal diode is shown in Figure 1.2.1 (d). As the forward voltage accross the diode tends to be greater than zero, the forward current through it tends to infinite. In practice, however, a diode is connected to other circuit elements, such as resistances, and its forward current is limited to a known value.

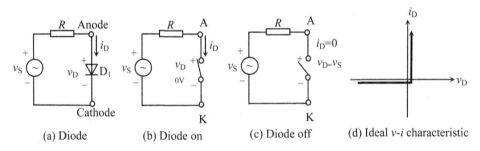

(a) Diode (b) Diode on (c) Diode off (d) Ideal v-i characteristic

Figure 1.2.1   Characteristic of An Ideal Diode

1.3 Practical Diodes

The characteristic of a practical diode that distinguishes it from an ideal one is that the practical diode experiences a finite voltage drop when it conducts. This drop is typically in the range of 0.5~0.7V. If the input voltage to a diode circuit is high enough; the drop is too small and can thus be ignored. The voltage drop may, however, cause a significant error in electronic circuits, and the diode characteristic should be taken into account in evaluating the performance of diode circuits. In order to understand the characteristic of a practical diode, we need to understand its physical operation.

1.4 Physical Operation of Junction Diodes

Junction diodes are made of semiconductor materials. A pure semiconductor is called an intrinsic material in which the concentrations of electrons n and holes p are equal. A hole is the absence of an electron in a covalent bond, and it is like an independent positive charge. The currents induced in pure semiconductors are very small. The most commonly used semiconductors are silicon, germanium, and gallium. Silicon materials cost less than germanium materials and allow diodes to operate at higher temperatures. For this reason, germanium diodes are rarely used any more. Gallium arsenide (GaAs) diodes can operate at higher switching speeds and higher frequencies than silicon diodes, and hence are preferable. However, gallium arsenide materials are more expensive than silicon materials, and gallium arsenide diodes are more difficult to manufacture, so they are generally used only for high-frequency applications. GaAs devices are expected to become increasingly important in electronic circuits.

To increase conductivity, controlled quantities of materials known as impurities are incorporated into pure semiconductors, creating free electrons or holes. The process of adding carefully controlled amounts of impurities to pure semiconductors is known as doping. A semiconductor to which impurities have been added is referred to as extrinsic. Two types of impurities are normally used: n-type, such as antimony, phosphorus, and arsenic; and p-type, such as boron, gallium, and indium.

1.4.1 Diode Junction

The n-type impurities are pentavalent materials, with five valence electrons in the outer shell of the atom. The addition of a controlled amount of an n-type impurity to silicon or germanium causes one electron to be very loosely attached to the parent atom, because four electrons are sufficient to complete a covalent bond. At room temperature, there is sufficient energy to cause the redundant electron to break away from its parent atom. Thus, a free electron is generated. This electron is free to move randomly within semiconductor crystal. Thus, an n-type impurity donates free electron to the semiconductor; for this reason, it is often referred to as a donor impurity. The impurity atom was originally neutral, and the removal of the redundant electron causes the impurity atom to exhibit a positive charge equal to +e and to remain fixed in the crystal lattice of the structure. An n-type semiconductor is shown in Figure 1.4.1 (a). Note that holes are also present in imperfect n-type semiconductor materials because of thermal agitations of electrons and holes within the materials. Therefore, in an n-type semiconductor, the electrons are the majority carriers and the holes are the minority carriers.

The p-type impurities are trivalent materials, with three valence electrons in the outer shell of the atom. The addition of a p-type impurity to silicon or germanium causes a vacancy for one electron in the vicinity of the impurity atom, because four electrons are necessary to complete covalent bonds. A vacancy for an electron is like a hole, which is equivalent to a positive charge +e. At room temperature, there is sufficient energy to cause a nearby electron to move into the existing vacancy, in turn causing a vacancy elsewhere. In this way, the hole moves randomly within the semiconductor crystal. Thus, a p-type impurity accepts free electrons and is referred to as an acceptor impurity. With the electron it gains, the impurity atom exhibits a charge of −e and remains fixed in crystal lattice of the structure. A p-type semiconductor is shown in Figure 1.4.1 (b). In a p-type semiconductor, the holes are the majority carriers and the electrons are the minority carriers.

To consider the principle of operation of a diode, we will assume that a p-type material is laid into one side of a single crystal of a pure semiconductor material, and an n-type material is laid into other side, as shown in Figure 1.4.1(c). At room temperature, the electrons, which are majority carriers in the n-region, diffuse from the n-type side to the p-type side; the holes, which are majority carriers in the p-region, diffuse from the p-type side to the n-type side. The electrons and holes will recombine near the junction and thus cancel each out. There will be opposite charges on each side of the junction, creating a depletion region, or space-charge region, as shown in Figure 1.4.1 (d). Under thermal equilibrium conditions, no more electrons or holes will cross the junction.

Because of the presence of opposite charges on each side of the junction, an electric field is established across the junction. The resultant potential barrier V_j, which arises because the n-type side is at a higher potential than the p-type side, prevents any flow of majority carriers to the other side. The variation of the potential across the junction is shown in Figure 1.4.1 (e).

Because of the potential barrier V_j, the electrons, which are minority carriers in the p-side, will be swept across the junction to the n-side; the holes, which are minority carriers in the n-side, will be swept across the junction to the p-side. Therefore, a current caused by the minority carriers (holes) will flow from the n-side to the p-side; it is known as the drift current I_{DR}. Similarly, a current known as the diffusion current I_{DF} will flow from the p-side to the n-side, caused by majority electrons. Under equilibrium conditions, the resultant current will be zero. Therefore, these two currents are equal, and flow in opposite directions. That is,

$$I_{DF} = -I_{DR}$$

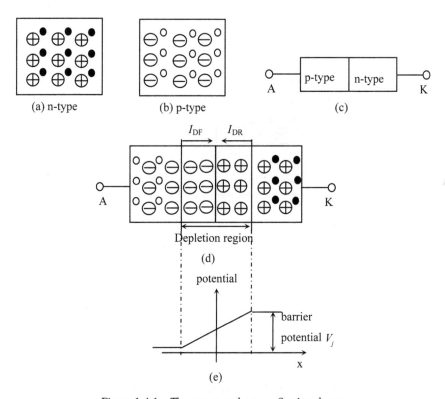

Figure 1.4.1 The n-type and p-type Semiconductor

1.4.2 Forward-Biased Condition

A junction is said to be forward-biased if the p-side is made positive with respect to the n-side, as depicted in Figure 1.4.2 (a). If the applied voltage v_D is increased, the potential barrier is reduced to $V_j - v_D$, as shown in Figure 1.4.2 (b), and a large number of holes flow from the p-side to the n-side. Similarly, a large number of electrons flow from the n-side to the p-side. The resultant diode current becomes $i_D = I_{DF} - I_{DR}$. As the diode current i_D increases, the ohmic resistances of p-side and the n-side cause a significant series voltage drop. If v_D is increased further, most of the increase in v_D will not be lost as a series voltage drop. Thus, the width of the depletion region reduced with the increase in the forward voltage. The potential barrier will not be reduced proportionally, but it can become zero.

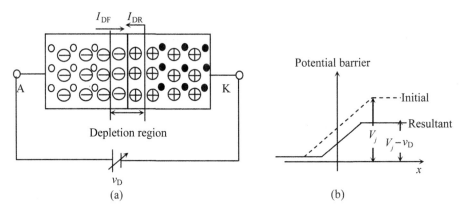

Figure 1.4.2 Forward-biased on Junctions

1.4.3 Reverse-Biased Condition

A junction is said to be reverse biased if the n-side is made positive with respect to the p-side, as depicted in Figure 1.4.3 (a). If the reverse voltage v_D is increased, the potential barrier is increased to $V_j + v_D$, as shown in Figure 1.4.3 (b). The holes from the p-side and the electrons from the n-side cannot cross the junction, and the diffusion current I_{DF} due to the majority carriers will be negligible. Because of a higher potential barrier, however, the minority holes in the n-side will be swept easily across the junction to the p-side; the minority electrons in the p-side will be swept easily across the junction to the n-side. Thus, the current will flow solely because of the minority carriers. The reverse current flow will be due to the drift current I_{DR}, which is known as the reverse saturation (or leakage) current, denoted by I_S as in Equation (1.5.1).

The number of minority carriers available is very small, and consequently the resulting current is also very small, on the order of microamperes. The production of minority carriers is dependent on the temperature. Thus, if the reverse voltage v_D is increased further, the diode current remains almost constant until a breakdown condition is reached. If the temperature increases, however, the reverse diode current also increases. The width of the depletion region is increased with an increase in the applied voltage.

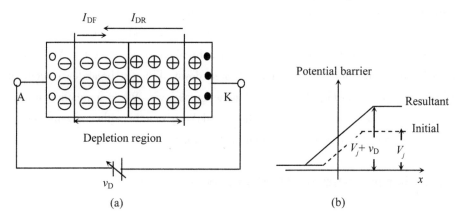

Figure 1.4.3 Reverse-biased on Junctions

1.4.4 Breakdown Condition

If the reverse voltage is kept sufficiently high, the electric field in the depletion layer will be strong enough to break the covalent bonds of silicon (or germanium) atoms, producing a large number of electron-hole pairs throughout the semiconductor crystal. These electrons and holes give rise to a large reverse current flow. The depletion region (often called the space-charge region) becomes so wide that collisions are less likely, but the even more intense electric field has the force to break the bonds directly. This phenomenon is called the tunneling effect or the zener effect. The mechanism is known as zener breakdown: Electrons and holes in turn cancel the negative and the positive charges of the depletion region, and the junction potential barrier is virtually removed. The reverse current is then limited by the external circuit only, while the reverse terminal voltage remains almost constant at the zener voltage V_Z.

When the high electric field becomes strong enough, the electrons in the p-side will be accelerated through the crystal and will collide with the unbroken covalent bonds with a force sufficient to break them. The electrons generated by the collisions may gain enough kinetic energy to strike other unbroken bonds with sufficient force to break them as well.

This cumulative effect, which will result in a large amount of uncontrolled current flow, is known as an avalanche breakdown.

In practice, the zener and avalanche effects are indistinguishable because both lead to a large reverse current. When a breakdown occur at $V_Z<5V$ (as in heavily doped junctions), it is a zener breakdown. When a breakdown occur at $V_Z>7V$ (approximated), it is an avalanche breakdown. When a junction breaks down at a voltage between $5\sim 7V$, the breakdown can be either a zener or an avalanche breakdown or a combination of the two.

1.5 Characteristics of Practical Diodes

The voltage-versus-current (v–i) characteristic of a practical diode is shown in Figure 1.5.1. This characteristic, which can be well approximated by an equation known as the Shockley diode equation, is given by

$$i_D = I_S(e^{\frac{v_D}{nV_T}}-1) \qquad (1.5.1)$$

where i_D—current through the diode, measured in amperes (A);

v_D—diode voltage with the anode positive with respect to the cathode, measured in volts (V);

I_S—leakage (or reverse saturation) current, typically in the range of

$10^{-6} \sim 10^{-5}$ A；

n—empirical constant known as the emission coefficient or the ideality factor, whose value varies from 1 to 2.

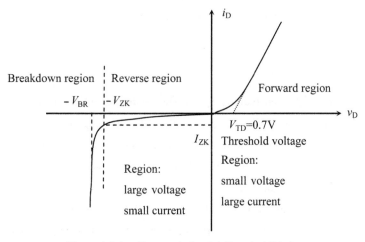

Figure 1.5.1 Characteristic of A Practical Diode

The emission coefficient n depends on the material and the physical construction of the diode. For germanium diodes, n is considered to be 1. For silicon diodes, the predicted value of n is 2 at very small or large currents, but for most practical silicon diodes, the value of n falls in the range of $1.1 \sim 1.8$.

V_T in Equation(1.5.1) is a constant called the thermal voltage, and it is given by

$$V_T = \frac{KT_K}{q} \tag{1.5.2}$$

where q—electron charge $= 1.6022 \times 10^{-19}$ coulomb (C);

T_K—absolute temperature in Kelvin $= 273 + T_{\text{celsius}}$;

K—Boltzmann's constant $= 1.3806 \times 10^{-23}$ J per Kelvin.

At a junction temperature of 25℃, Equation(1.5.1) gives the value of V_T as

$$V_T = \frac{KT_K}{q} = \frac{(1.3806 \times 10^{-23})(273+25)}{1.6022 \times 10^{-19}} = 25.8\text{mV}$$

At a special temperature, the leakage current I_S will remain constant for a given diode. For small-signal (or low power) diodes, the typical value of I_S is 10^{-9} A. We can divide the diode characteristic of Figure 1.5.1 into three regions, as follows:

Forward-biased region, where $v_D > 0$;
Reverse-biased region, where $v_D < 0$;
Breakdown region, where $v_D < -V_{ZK}$.

1.5.1 Forward-Biased Region

In the forward-biased region, $v_D > 0$. The diode current i_D will be very small if the diode voltage v_D is less than a specific value V_{TD}, known as the threshold voltage or the cut-in voltage or the turn-on voltage (typically 0.7V). The diode conducts fully if v_D is higher than V_{TD}. Thus, the threshold voltage is the voltage at which a forward-biased diode begins to conduct.

Assume that a small forward voltage of $v_D = 0.1$V is applied to a diode of $n = 1$, at room temperature, $V_T = 25.8$mV. From Equation (1.5.1), We can find the diode current i_D as $i_D = I_S(e^{\frac{v_D}{nV_T}} - 1) = I_S(e^{\frac{0.1}{1 \times 0.0258}} - 1) = I_S(48.23 - 1) \approx 48.23 I_S$ with 2.1% error. Therefore, for $v_D > 0.1$V, which is usually the case, $i_D \gg I_S$, and Equation (1.5.1) can be approximated within 2.1% error by

$$i_D = I_S(e^{\frac{v_D}{nV_T}} - 1) \approx I_S e^{\frac{v_D}{nV_T}} \qquad (1.5.3)$$

1.5.2 Reverse-Biased Region

In the reverse-biased region, $v_D < 0$. That is, v_D is negative. If $|v_D| \gg V_T$, which occurs for $v_D < -0.1$V, the exponential term in Equation (1.5.1) becomes negligibly small compared to unity and the diode current i_D becomes

$$i_D = I_S(e^{\frac{v_D}{nV_T}} - 1) = -I_S \qquad (1.5.4)$$

which indicates that the diode current i_D remains constant in the reverse direction and is equal to I_S in magnitude.

1.5.3 Breakdown Region

In the breakdown region, the reverse voltage is high—usually greater than 100V. If the magnitude of the reverse voltage exceeds a specified voltage known as the breakdown voltage V_{BR}, the corresponding reverse current I_{BV} increases rapidly for a small change in reverse voltage beyond V_{BR}. Operation in the breakdown region will not be destructive to the diode provided the power dissipation is kept within the safe level specified in the manufacture's data sheet. It is often necessary, however, to limit the reverse current in the breakdown region so that the power dissipation falls within a permissible range.

1.6 Zener Diodes

If the reverse voltage of a diode exceeds a specific voltage called the breakdown voltage, the diode will operate in the breakdown region. In this region, the reverse diode current rises very rapidly. The diode voltage remains almost constant and is independent of the diode current. However, operation in the breakdown region will not be destructive if the diode current is limited to a safe value by an external circuitry so that the power dissipation within the diode is within permissible limits specified by the manufacturer and it does not overheat.

A diode especially designed to have a very steep characteristic in the breakdown region is called a zener diode. The symbol for a zener diode is shown in Figure 1.6.1 (b) and its v-i characteristic in Figure 1.6.1 (b). V_{ZK} is the knee voltage, and I_{ZK} is the corresponding current. A zener diode is specified by its breakdown voltage, called the zener voltage (or reference voltage) V_Z, at a specified test current $I_Z = I_{ZT}$. $I_{z(max)}$ is the maximum current that the zener diode can withstand and still remain within permissible limits for power dissipation. $I_{z(min)}$ is the minimum current, slightly below the knee of the characteristic curve, at which the diode exhibits the reverse breakdown.

In the forward direction, the zener diode behaves like a normal diode; its equivalent circuit is shown in Figure 1.6.1 (c). In the reverse direction, it offers a very high resistance, acting like a normal reverse-biased diode if $|v_D| < V_Z$, and like a low-resistance diode if $|v_D| > V_Z$. For example, let us consider a zener diode with nominal voltage $V_Z = 5V \pm 2V$. For $3V < |v_D| < 5V$ in the reverse direction, the diode will normally exhibit a zener effect. For $5V < V_Z < 7V$, the breakdown could be due to the zener effect, the avalanche effect, or a combination of the two.

Chapter 1 Diodes and Applications

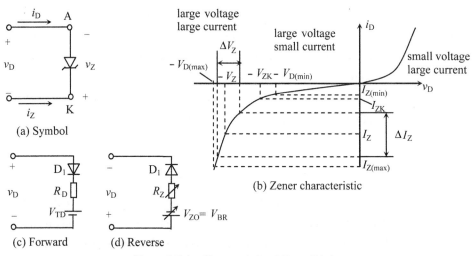

Figure 1.6.1 Characteristic of Zener Diode

The reverse (zener) characteristic of Figure 1.6.1 (b) can be approximated by a piecewise linear model with a fixed voltage V_{Z0} and an ideal diode in series with resistance R_Z. The equivalent circuit of the zener action is shown in Figure 1.6.1 (d) for $|v_D| > V_Z$. R_Z depends on the inverse slope of the zener characteristic and is defined as

$$R_Z = \frac{\Delta V_Z}{\Delta I_Z}\bigg|V_Z = \frac{\Delta v_D}{\Delta i_D}\bigg|, \quad \text{for } v_D < 0 \text{ and } i_D < 0$$

R_Z is also called the zener resistance. The value of R_Z remains almost constant over a wide range of the zener characteristic. However, its value changes very rapidly in the vicinity of the knee point. Thus, a zener diode should be operated away from the knee point. The typical value of R_Z is a few tens of ohms, but it increases with current i_D. At the knee point of the zener characteristic, R_Z has a high value, typically 3kΩ. The zener current $i_Z(=-i_D)$ can be related to V_{Z0} and R_Z by $V_Z = V_{Z0} + R_Z i_Z$.

A zener diode may be regarded as offering a variable resistance whose value changes with the current so that the voltage drop across the terminals remains constant. Therefore, it is also known as a voltage reference diode. The value of R_Z is very small. Thus, the zener voltage V_Z is almost independent of the reverse diode current $i_D = -i_Z$. Because of the constant voltage characteristic in the breakdown region, a zener diode can be employed as a voltage regulator. A regulator maintains an almost constant output voltage even though the dc supply voltage and the load current may vary over a wide range. A zener voltage regulator is shown in Figure 1.6.2. A zener voltage regulator is also known as a shunt regulator because the zener diode is connected in shunt (or parallel) with the load R_L. The value of resistance R_S should be such that the diode can operate in the breakdown region over the entire range of input voltages v_S and variations of the current i_L.

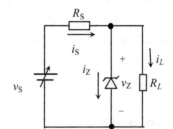

Figure 1.6.2 Zener Shunt Regulator

1.7 Light-Emitting Diodes

A light-emitting diode (LED) is a special type of semiconductor diode that emits light when it is forward biased. The light intensity is approximately proportional to the forward diode current i_D. Light-emitting diodes are normally used in low-cost applications such as calculators, cameras, appliances, and automobile instrument panels.

1.8 Applications of Diodes

We have seen that a diode offers a very low resistance in one direction and a very high resistance in the other direction, thus permitting an easy current flow in only one direction. The section will illustrate the applications of diodes in wave-shaping circuits. For the sake of simplicity, we will assume ideal diodes—that is, diodes in which the voltage drop across the diode is zero, rather than the typical value of 0.7 V.

1.8.1 Diode Rectifiers

The most common applications of diodes are known as rectifiers. A rectifier that converts an ac voltage to a unidirectional voltage is used as a dc power supply for many electronic circuits, such as those in radios, calculators, and stereo amplifiers. A rectifier is also called an ac-dc converter. Rectifiers can be classified on the basis of ac input supply into two types: single-phase rectifiers, in which the ac input voltage is a single-phase source, and three-phase rectifiers, in which the ac input voltage is a three-phase source. Three-phase rectifiers, which are normally used in high-power applications, are beyond the scope of this text. The following single-phase rectifiers are commonly used in electronic circuits: single-phase half-wave rectifiers, single-phase full-wave center-tapped rectifiers, and single-phase full-wave bridge rectifiers.

1. Single-phase half-wave rectifiers

The circuit diagram of a single-phase half-wave rectifier is shown in Figure 1.8.1 (a). Let us consider a sinusoidal input voltage $v_S = V_m \sin\omega t$, where $\omega = 2\pi ft$, and f is the frequency of the input voltage. Since v_S is positive from $\omega t = 0 \sim \pi$ and negative from $\omega t = \pi \sim 2\pi$, the operation of the rectifier can be divided into two intervals: interval 1 and interval 2.

Interval 1 is the interval $0 \leqslant \omega t \leqslant \pi$ during the positive half-cycle of the input voltage. Diode D_1 conducts and behaves like a short circuit, as shown in Figure 1.8.1 (b). The output voltage appears across the load resistance R_L. That is, the output voltage becomes

$$v_o = V_m \sin\omega t \quad \text{for} \quad 0 \leqslant \omega t \leqslant \pi$$

Interval 2 is the interval $\pi \leqslant \omega t \leqslant 2\pi$ during the negative half-cycle of the input voltage. Diode D_1 is reverse biased and behaves like an open circuit, as shown in Figure 1.8.1 (b). The output voltage v_o becomes zero. That is,

$$v_o = 0, \quad \text{for} \quad \pi \leqslant \omega t \leqslant 2\pi$$

The waveforms of the input voltage, the output voltage, and the diode voltage are shown in Figure 1.8.1 (c). When diode D_1 conducts, its voltage becomes zero. When the diode is reverse biased, the diode current becomes zero and the diode has to withstand the input voltage. The peak inverse voltage (PIV) the diode must withstand is equal to the peak input voltage V_m. The voltage on the anode side of

1.8 Applications of Diodes   21

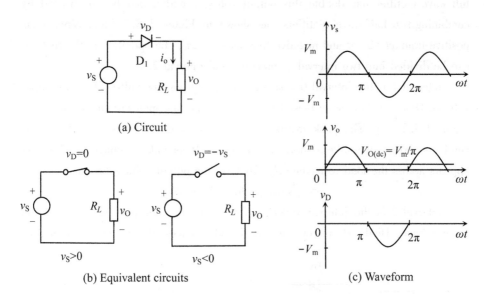

Figure 1.8.1   Single-phase Half-wave Rectifiers

the diode is ac, whereas on the cathode side it is dc. That is, the diode converts ac voltage to dc. The average output voltage $V_{O(dc)}$ is found using the following equation:

$$V_{O(dc)} = \frac{1}{2\pi}\int_0^\pi v_o d(\omega t) = \frac{V_m}{\pi} = 0.318 V_m \qquad (1.8.1)$$

Therefore, the average load current $I_{O(dc)}$ for a resistive load can be found from

$$I_{O(dc)} = \frac{V_{O(dc)}}{R_L} = \frac{V_m}{\pi R_L} = \frac{0.318}{R_L} \qquad (1.8.2)$$

The rms output voltage $V_{O(rms)}$ is given by

$$V_{O(rms)} = \left[\frac{1}{2\pi}\int_0^\pi v_o{}^2 d(\omega t)\right]^{\frac{1}{2}} = \frac{V_m}{2} = 0.5 V_m \qquad (1.8.3)$$

and the rms load current $I_{O(rms)}$ is given by

$$I_{O(rms)} = \frac{V_{O(rms)}}{R_L} = \frac{0.5 V_m}{R_L} \qquad (1.8.4)$$

2. Single-Phase Full-wave Center-Tapped Rectifiers

For a half-wave rectifier, the average (or dc) voltage is only 0.318 V_m. A

Chapter 1 Diodes and Applications

full-wave rectifier has double this output voltage, and it can be constructed by combining two half-wave rectifiers, as shown in Figure 1.8.2 (a). Since v_S is positive from $\omega t = 0 \sim \pi$ and negative from $\omega t = \pi \sim 2\pi$, the operation of the rectifier can be divided into two intervals: interval 1 and interval 2.

Interval 1 is the interval $0 \leqslant \omega t \leqslant \pi$ during the positive half-cycle of the input voltage. Diode D_2 is reverse biased and behaves like an open circuit, as shown in Figure 1.8.2 (b). The peak inverse voltage PIV of diode D_2 is $2V_m$. Diode D_1 conducts and behaves like a short circuit. The half-secondary voltage $v_S = V_m \sin\omega t$ appears across the load resistance R_L. That is, the output voltage becomes

$$v_O = V_m \sin\omega t, \quad \text{for} \quad 0 \leqslant \omega t \leqslant \pi$$

Interval 2 is the interval $\pi \leqslant \omega t \leqslant 2\pi$ during the negative half-cycle of the input voltage. Diode D_1 is reverse-biased and behaves like an open circuit, as

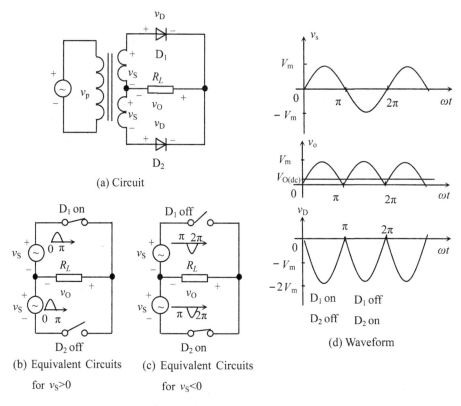

Figure 1.8.2 Full-wave Rectifiers with a Center-tapped Transform

shown in Figure 1.8.2(b). The peak inverse voltage PIV of diode D_1 is also $2V_m$. Diode D_2 conducts and behaves like a short circuit. The negative of the half-secondary voltage $v_S = V_m \sin\omega t$ appears across the load resistance R_L. That is, the output voltage becomes

$$v_O = -V_m \sin\omega t, \quad \text{for} \quad \pi \leqslant \omega t \leqslant 2\pi$$

The instantaneous output voltage v_O during interval 2 is identical to that for interval 1. The waveforms for the input and output voltages are shown in Figure 1.8.2 (d). The average output voltage $V_{O(dc)}$ can be found from the following equation:

$$V_{O(dc)} = \frac{2}{2\pi} \int_0^\pi v_O d(\omega t) = \frac{2V_m}{\pi} = 0.636 V_m \quad (1.8.5)$$

It is twice the average output voltage of a half-wave rectifier, $V_{O(dc)} = 0.318 V_m$.

Therefore the average load current $I_{O(dc)}$ for a resistance load can be found:

$$I_{O(dc)} = \frac{V_{O(dc)}}{R_L} = \frac{2V_m}{\pi R_L} = \frac{0.636 V_m}{R_L} \quad (1.8.6)$$

The rms output voltage $V_{O(rms)}$ is given by

$$V_{O(rms)} = \left[\frac{2}{2\pi} \int_0^\pi v_O^2 d(\omega t) \right]^{\frac{1}{2}} = \frac{V_m}{\sqrt{2}} = 0.707 V_m \quad (1.8.7)$$

compared to $V_{O(rms)} = 0.5 V_m$ for a half-wave rectifier. Therefore, the rms load current $I_{O(rms)}$ is given by

$$I_{O(rms)} = \frac{V_{O(rms)}}{R_L} = \frac{0.707 V_m}{R_L} \quad (1.8.8)$$

3. Single-Phase Full-Wave Bridge Rectifier

A single-phase full-wave bridge rectifier is shown in Figure 1.8.3 (a). It requires four diodes. The advantages of this rectifier are that it requires no transformer at the input side and the PIV rating of the diodes is V_m. The disadvantages are that it does not provide electrical isolation and it requires more diodes than the center-tapped version. However, an input transformer is normally used to satisfy the output voltage requirement. Since v_S is positive from $0 \leqslant \omega t \leqslant \pi$ and negative from $\pi \leqslant \omega t \leqslant 2\pi$, the circuit operation can be divided into two intervals: interval 1 and interval 2.

Interval 1 is the interval $0 \leqslant \omega t \leqslant \pi$ during the positive half-cycle of the input voltage v_S. Diodes D_3 and D_4 are reverse biased, as shown in Figure 1.8.3 (b). The peak inverse voltage PIV of diodes D_3 and D_4 is V_m. Diodes D_1 and D_2 conduct. The input voltage $v_S = V_m \sin\omega t$ appears across the load resistance R_L. That is, the output voltage becomes

$$v_O = -V_m \sin\omega t, \quad \text{for} \quad \pi \leqslant \omega t \leqslant 2\pi$$

The waveforms for the input and output voltages are shown in Figure 1.8.3 (d). The output ripple voltage is shown in Figure 1.8.3 (e). The equations that were derived earlier for a single phase full-wave center-tapped transformer are also valid for the bridge rectifier.

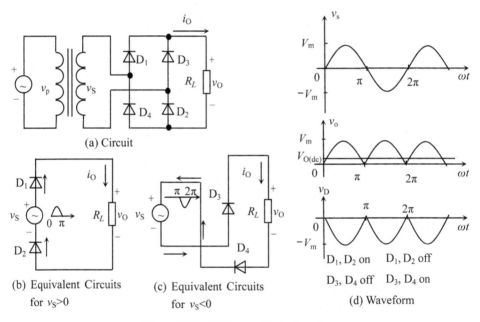

Figure 1.8.3 Full-wave Bridge Rectifiers

1.8.2 Clippers

A clipper is a limiting circuit; it is basically an extension of the half-wave rectifier. The output of a clipper circuit looks as if a portion of the output signal was cut off (clipped). Although the input voltage can have any waveform, we will

1.8 Applications of Diodes 25

assume that the input voltage is sinusoidal, $v_s = V_m \sin\omega t$, in order to describe the output voltage. Clippers can be classified into two types: parallel clippers and series clippers.

1. Parallel Clippers

A clipper in which the diode is connected across the output terminals is known as a parallel clipper, because the diode will be in parallel (or shunt) with the load. In a shunt connection, elements are connected in parallel such that each element carries a different current. Some examples of parallel clipper circuits and their corresponding output waveforms are shown in Figure 1.8.4. The resistance R limits the diode current when the diode conducts. The diode can be connected either in series or in parallel with the load. In determining the output waveform of a

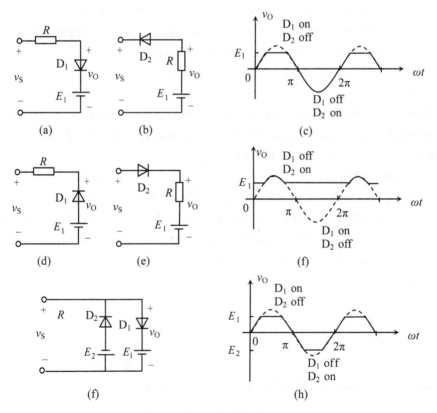

Figure 1.8.4 Parallel Clippers

clipper, it is important to keep in mind that a diode will conduct only if the anode voltage is higher than the cathode voltage.

When diode D_1 in Figure 1.8.4 (a) is off, the instantaneous output voltage v_O equals the instantaneous input voltage v_S. Diode D_1 will conduct for the position of the positive half-cycle during which the instantaneous input voltage v_S is higher than the battery voltage E_1. On the other hand, diode D_2 in Figure 1.8.4(b) will conduct when the input voltage is less than the battery voltage E_1. Although the output waveforms of these two circuits are identical, as shown in Figure 1.8.4(c), diode D_2 in Figure 1.8.4(b) remains on for a longer time than diode D_1 in Figure 1.8.4(a). For this reason, the clipper of Figure 1.8.4(a) is preferable to that of Figure 1.8.4(b).

Diode D_1 in Figure 1.8.4 (d) will conduct most of the time and be off for the portion of the positive half-cycle during which the instantaneous input voltage v_S is higher than battery voltage E_1. The output waveforms for the clippers of Figure 1.8.4(d) and 1.8.4(e) identical, as shown in Figure 1.8.4(f).

The circuits of Figure 1.8.4 (a) and 1.8.4 (d) (with E_1 reversed and renamed as E_2) can be combined to form a two-level clipper, as shown in Figure 1.8.4 (g). The positive and negative voltages are limited to E_1 and E_2, respectively, as shown in Figure 1.8.4 (h). One battery terminal of the clippers in Figure 1.8.4 is common to the ground.

2.Series Clippers

A clipper in which the diode is series with the output terminals is known as a series clipper. The current-limiting resistance R can be used as a load, as shown in Figure 1.8.5(a). If the direction of the battery is reversed, the negative part of the sine wave is clipped as shown in Figure 1.8.5(b). If the direction of the diode is reversed, the clipping becomes the opposite of that in Figure 1.8.5(a); this situation is shown in Figure 1.8.5(c). The potential difference between terminals A and B of the battery must be E_1. But terminal B cannot be at zero or ground potential. Therefore, these circuits require an isolated dc voltage (or battery) of E_1. Note that the zero level of the output voltage v_O is different from that of the input voltage v_S and is shifted by an amount equal to E_1.

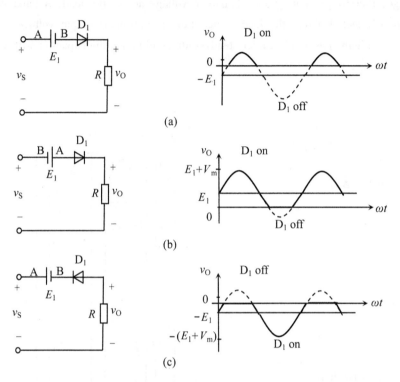

Figure 1.8.5 Series Clippers

1.8.3 Output Filters for Rectifiers

The rectifier output voltage has a dc component $\left(\dfrac{V_m}{\pi} \text{ or } \dfrac{2V_m}{\pi}\right)$ and other cosine components at various frequencies. The magnitudes of the cosine components are called the harmonics. The output should ideally be pure dc; these harmonics are undesirable. Filters are normally used to smooth out the output voltage. Since the input supply to these filters is dc, they are known as dc filters. Three types of dc filters are normally used: L-filters, C-filters, and LC-filters, and they are generally used for high-power applications, such as dc power supplies. In integrated circuits, C-filters are usually used.

A capacitor is an energy storage element; it tries to maintain a constant voltage, thereby preventing any change in voltage across the load. A capacitor C can be connected across the load to maintain a continuous output voltage v_O, as shown in Figure 1.8.6(a). Under steady-state conditions, the capacitor will have a finite voltage.

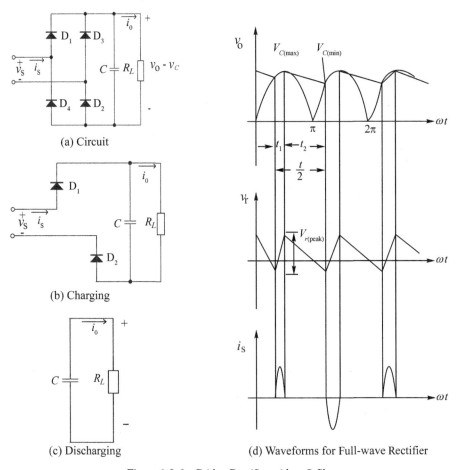

Figure 1.8.6 Bridge Rectifier with a C-filter

When the magnitude of the instantaneous supply voltage v_S is greater than that of the instantaneous capacitor voltage v_C, the diodes (D_1 and D_2 or D_3 and D_4) will conduct and the capacitor will be charged from the supply. However, if the magnitude of the voltage v_S falls below that of the instantaneous capacitor voltage

v_C, the diodes (D_1 and D_2 or D_3 and D_4) will be reverse-biased and the capacitor C will discharge through the load resistance R_L. The capacitor voltage v_C will vary between a minimum value $v_{C(\min)}$ and a maximum value $v_{C(\max)}$. The waveforms of the output voltage v_O and ripple voltage v_r are shown in Figure 1.8.6(b). If f is the supply frequency, the period of the input voltage is $T = \dfrac{1}{f}$.

For a single-phase half-wave rectifier, the period of the output ripple voltage is the same as the period T of the supply voltage. However, for a single-phase full-wave rectifier, the period of the output ripple voltage is $\dfrac{T}{2}$. In order to derive an explicit expression for the ripple factor RF of the output voltage, let us assume the following:

(1) t_1 is the charging time of the capacitor C.

(2) t_2 is the discharging time of the capacitor C.

$$t_1 + t_2 = \begin{cases} \dfrac{T}{2}, & \text{for a full-wave rectifier,} \\ T, & \text{for a half-wave rectifier.} \end{cases}$$

(3) The charging time t_1 is very small compared to the discharging time t_2. That is, generally $t_2 \gg t_1$, and more specifically,

$$t_2 = \dfrac{T}{2} - t_1 \approx \dfrac{T}{2}, \quad \text{for a full-wave rectifier,}$$

$$t_2 \approx T, \quad \text{for a half-wave rectifier.}$$

The equivalent circuit during charging is shown in Figure 1.8.6(c). The capacitor charges almost instantaneously to the supply voltage v_S. The capacitor C will be charged approximately to the peak supply voltage V_m, so $v_C(t = t_1) = V_m$. Figure 1.8.6(d) shows the equivalent circuit during discharging. The capacitor discharges exponentially through R_L. When one of the diode pairs is conducting, the capacitor C draws a pulse of charging current from the ac supply, as shown in Figure 1.8.6(e). As a result, the rectifier generates harmonic currents into the ac supply. For high-power applications, an input filter is normally required to reduce the amount of harmonic injection into the ac supply. Thus, a rectifier with a C-filter is used only for low-power applications.

By redefining the time origin ($t = 0$) as the beginning of interval 1, we can deduce the discharging current from

$$\frac{1}{C}\int i_0 dt - v_C(t=0) + R_L i_0 = 0 \quad (1.8.9)$$

which, with an initial condition of $v_C(t=t_1) = V_m$, gives

$$i_0 = \frac{V_m}{R_L} e^{\frac{-(t-t_1)}{R_L C}} \quad \text{for } t_1 \leq t \leq (t_1 + t_2) \quad (1.8.10)$$

The instantaneous output (or capacitor) voltage v_O during the discharging period can be found from

$$v_O(t) = R_L i_0 = V_m e^{\frac{-(t-t_1)}{R_L C}} \quad (1.8.11)$$

The peak-to-peak ripple voltage $V_{r(pp)}$ can be found from

$$V_{r(pp)} = v_O(t=t_1) - v_O(t=t_1+t_2) = V_m - V_m e^{\frac{-t_2}{R_L C}} = V_m(1 - e^{\frac{-t_2}{R_L C}}) \quad (1.8.12)$$

Since $e^{-x} \approx 1 - x$, Equation (1.8.12) can be simplified to

$$V_{r(pp)} = \begin{cases} V_m\left(1 - 1 + \dfrac{t_2}{R_L C}\right) = \dfrac{V_m t_2}{R_L C} = \dfrac{V_m}{2fR_L C}, & \text{for a full-wave rectifier} \\ \dfrac{V_m}{fR_L C}, & \text{for a half-wave rectifier} \end{cases}$$

Therefore, the average output voltage $V_{O(dc)}$ is given by

$$V_{O(dc)} = \begin{cases} V_m - \dfrac{V_{r(pp)}}{2} = V_m - \dfrac{V_m}{4fR_L C} = \dfrac{V_m(4fR_L C - 1)}{4fR_L C}, & \text{for a full-wave rectifier} \\ V_m - \dfrac{V_m}{2fR_L C} = \dfrac{V_m(2fR_L C - 1)}{2fR_L C}, & \text{for a half-wave rectifier} \end{cases}$$

usually,

$$fR_L C = \frac{1}{2}(3 \sim 5)$$

so we can get

$$V_{O(dc)} \approx 1.2 V_2 \quad (1.8.13)$$

where, $V_2 = \dfrac{V_m}{\sqrt{2}}$.

Let us assume that the ripple voltage is approximately a sine wave. In that case the rms ripple voltage $V_{r(rms)}$ of the output voltage can be found by dividing the peak ripple voltage by $\sqrt{2}$:

$$V_{r(rms)} = \begin{cases} \dfrac{V_{r(pp)}}{2\sqrt{2}} = \dfrac{V_m}{4\sqrt{2}fR_LC}, & \text{for a full-wave rectifier,} \\ \dfrac{V_m}{2\sqrt{2}fR_LC}, & \text{for a half-wave rectifier.} \end{cases}$$

The ripple factor RF of the output voltage can be found as follows:

$$RF = \dfrac{V_{r(rms)}}{V_{O(dc)}} = \dfrac{V_m}{4\sqrt{2}fR_LC} \times \dfrac{4fR_LC}{V_m(4fR_LC-1)} = \dfrac{1}{\sqrt{2}(4fR_LC-1)}$$

$$= \begin{cases} \dfrac{1}{\sqrt{2}(4fR_LC-1)}, & \text{for a full-wave rectifier,} \\ \dfrac{1}{\sqrt{2}(2fR_LC-1)}, & \text{for a half-wave rectifier.} \end{cases} \quad (1.8.14)$$

Summary

A diode is a two-terminal semiconductor device. It offers a very low resistance in the forward direction and a very high resistance in the reverse direction. In a zener diode, the reverse breakdown is controlled, and the zener voltage is the breakdown voltage. Diodes are used in many electronic circuits, including those of rectifiers, battery chargers, clippers, clampers, peak demodulators, voltage multipliers, function generation, logic gate, and voltage regulators. The analysis of diode circuits can be simplified by assuming an ideal diode model in which the resistance in the forward-biased condition is zero and the resistance in the reverse direction is very large, approaching infinity.

Problems

1.1 Describe in your own words the meaning of the word ideal as applied to a device or system.

1.2 Describe in your own words the characteristics of the ideal diode and how they determine the on and off states of the device. That is, describe why the short-circuit and open-circuit equivalents are appropriate.

1.3 What is the one important different between the characteristics of a simple switch and those of an ideal diode?

1.4 (a) Using the approximate characteristics for the Si diode, determine the level of V_D, I_D, and V_R for the circuit of Figure p1.4.

(b) Perform the same analysis as part (a) using the ideal model for the diode.

(c) Do the results obtained in parts (a) and (b) suggest that the ideal model can provide a good approximation for the actual response under some conditions?

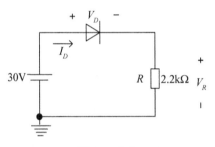

Figure p1.4

1.5 Determine V_O and I_D for the networks of Figure p1.5.

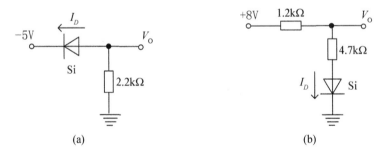

Figure p1.5

1.6 Assuming an ideal diode, skectch v_i, v_d, and i_d for the half-wave rectifier of Figure p1.6. The input is a wave form with a frequency of 60Hz.

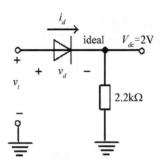

Figure p1.6

1.7 Repeat problem 1.6 with a 6.8kΩ load applied as shown in Figure p1.7.

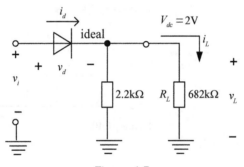

Figure p1.7

1.8 A full-wave bridge rectifier with a 120-Vrms sinusoidal input has a load resistor of 1kΩ.

(a) If silicon diodes are employed, what is the dc voltage available at the load?

(b) Determine the required PIV rating of each diode.

(c) Find the maximum current through each diode during conduction.

(d) What is the required power rating of each diode?

1.9 Determine v_o for each network of Figure p.1.9 for the input shown.

Chapter 1 Diodes and Applications

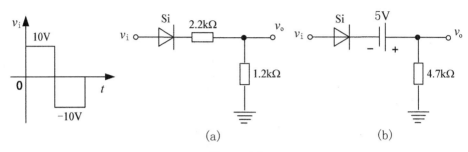

Figure p1.9

1.10 Sketch i_R and v_o for the network of Figure p1.10 for the input shown.

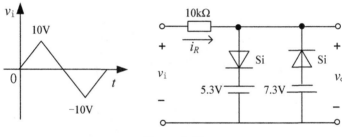

Figure p1.10

Chapter 2
Amplifiers

The output signals from transducers are weak [in the range of microvolts (μV) or millivolts (mV)] and possess a very small amount of energy. These signals are generally too small in magnitude to be processed reliably to perform any useful function. Signal processing is much easier if the magnitude of the signal is large (in the range of volts). Amplifiers are used in almost every electronic system to increase the strength of a weak signal. An amplifier consists of one or more amplifying devices. The complexity of an amplifier depends on the number of amplifying devices. Internally, amplifiers use one or more transistors as amplifying devices, and these transistors are biased from a single dc supply to operate properly at a desired Q-point. Using transistors, we can build amplifiers that give a voltage gain, a high input impedance, or a high output impedance. The terminal behavior of an amplifier depends on the types of devices used within the amplifier.

Transistors are the key components of amplifiers. Although there are various types of transistors, we can classify them broadly into two types: bipolar junction transistors and field-effect transistors. Transistors are active devices with strongly nonlinear characteristics. Thus, in order to analyze and design a transistor circuit, we need models of transistors. Creating accurate models requires a very good knowledge of the physical operation of transistors and their parameters as well as a powerful analytical technique. A circuit can be analyzed easily using simple models, but there is generally a trade-off between accuracy and complexity. A simple model, however, is always useful to obtain the approximate values of circuit elements for the design exercise and the approximate performance of the element for circuit evaluation. In this chapter, we will consider the operation and external characteristics of bipolar junction transistors and field-effect transistors using simple linear models.

2.1 Bipolar Junction Transistor

The bipolar junction transistor (BJT), developed in the 1960s, is the first device for amplification of signals. It consists of a silicon (or germanium) crystal to which impurities have been added such that a layer of p-type (or n-type) silicon is sandwiched between two layers of n-type (or p-type) silicon. Therefore, there are two types of transistors: npn and pnp. The basic structures of npn and pnp transistors are shown in Figure 2.1.1 (a) and (b). A BJT may be viewed as two pn junctions connected back to back. It is called bipolar because two polarity carriers (holes and electrons) carry charges in the device. A BJT is often referred to simply as a transistor. It has three terminals, known as the emitter (E), the base (B), and the collector (C), respectively. Pn junction between emitting region and base region is emitting junction and pn junction between collecting region and base region is collecting junction. The symbols are shown in Figure 2.1.1(c) and (d). The direction of the arrow by the emitter determines whether the transistor is an npn or a pnp transistor.

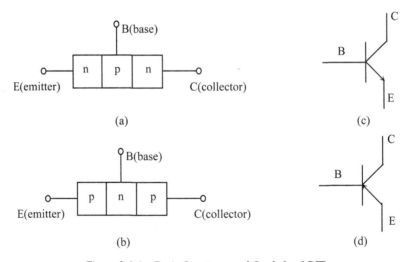

Figure 2.1.1 Basic Structures and Symbols of BJTs

2.1 Bipolar Junction Transistor

The important characteristics of the BJT structure are:

The emitting region and collecting region are of same type of semiconductor but the emitting region is of heavy impurity with high density and the collecting region is of light impurity with low density. In addition both are not the same in physical dimension of the emitting region is smaller than that of the collecting region.

The base region is very thin and the impurity is light.

2.1.1 Principle

There are two different types of BJT, i.e. npn & pnp, but their principles are almost the same. The differences are that the external voltage and the current direction for all the electrodes of npn and pnp are reverse.

Figure 2.1.2(a) and (b) show the circuit diagram of npn & pnp. In order for the triode (BJT) to have amplifying function, directional voltage should be applied across the emitting junction and the reverse voltage should be applied across the collecting junction, i.e. $V_C > V_B > V_E$ for npn, $V_E > V_B > V_C$ for npn. It is known that applied across the emitter current I_E, the base current I_B and the collector current I_C have the following relationship:

$$I_E = I_B + I_C.$$

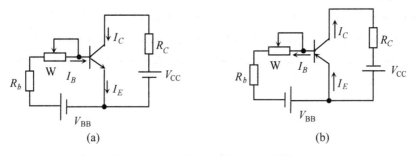

Figure 2.1.2 Circuit Diagram of BJTs

If the potentiometer W is adjusted, There would be some changes in I_B and I_C and the currents on all the electrodes by means of measurement are shown in Table 2.1.1.

Table 2.1.1

	1	2	3	4
$I_B(\mu A)$	10	28	40	65
$I_C(mA)$	0.99	1.97	2.96	4.94

The micro change of the I_B can make the big change of the I_C. The controlling function of this kind is called current amplifying function of the BJT.

2.1.2 Input and Output Characteristics

A transistor must be biased in order to properly initiate current flow. Figure 2.1.2 illustrates this biasing using two dc supplies, V_{CC} and V_{BB}. This arrangement is not used in practice; it is shown only to illustrate the transistor characteristics. A practical biasing circuit uses only one dc supply for transistor biasing; this arrangement is discussed later in section 2.1.3. R_c serves as a load resistance.

Each of the three terminals of a transistor may serve as an input terminal, an output terminal, or a common terminal. There are three possible configurations as shown in Figure 2.1.3. For common emitter (CE) in Figure 2.1.3(a), the base is input terminal, the collector is output terminal, and the emitter is the common terminal; For common collector (CC) or emitter follower in Figure 2.1.3(b), the collector is the common terminal; For common base (CB) in Figure 2.1.3(c), the base is the common terminal. The CB configuration is not as commonly used as the other two. A transistor can be described by two characteristics: input characteristic and output characteristic.

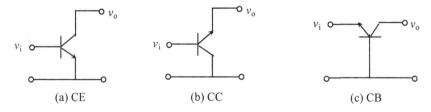

Figure 2.1.3 Three Possible Configurations

1. Input Characteristics

When the voltage v_{CE} between the collector and the emitter is unchanged, the relationship between the base current i_B and the base voltage v_{BE} is called the input characteristic of a transistor.

The input characteristic is similar to that of a forward-biased diode if the emitter is the common terminal; the input characteristic for npn and pnp transistors is shown in Figure 2.1.4(a). It also has a section of dead area voltage. The value of it for silicon is 0.7V and for germanium is 0.2V.

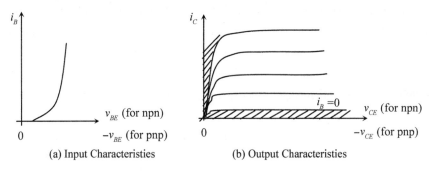

(a) Input Characteristies (b) Output Characteristies

Figure 2.1.4 Input and Output Characteristics

2. Output Characteristic

When the base current i_B is constant, the relation between the collector voltage v_{CE} and the collector current i_C is called output characteristic of a transistor.

A typical output characteristic for a BJT is shown in Figure 2.1.4(b). v_{CE} and i_C are positive for npn transistors and negative for pnp transistors. The output characteristic may be divided into three regions: an active region, a saturation region, and a cutoff region.

1) Active region

In the active region, $0 < v_{BE} < v_{CE}$ and $v_{CB}(=v_{CE}-v_{BE}) > 0$; that is, the emitter junction is forward biased and the collecting junction is reverse biased. A small change in i_B can cause a great change in i_C and the change in i_C is not related to the v_{CE}. i_C is only controlled by i_B, $i_C = \beta i_B$. β is current amplifying coefficient. The triode has the current amplifying function when it operates in this region. Therefore this region is called amplifying region. All transistors exhibit high output resistance. Operation in the active region can give an amplification of signals with a minimum amount of distortion, because the output characteristic is approximately linear.

A transistor is a current-controlled device. β is defined as

$$\beta = \frac{i_C}{i_B} \qquad (2.1.1)$$

its value typically ranges from 50 to 350.

2) Saturation region

In the saturation region, emitter junction is forward biased and $v_{BE} \approx 0.7\text{V}$. The collecting junction is also forward biased. If the base current i_B is kept constant, then the collector current i_C will increase with the voltage v_{CE} until the collector current saturates that is, it reaches a level at which any increase in v_{CE} causes no significant change in the collector current. The transistor can be used as a switch in the saturation region, because v_{CE} is low, typically 0.3V.

3) Cut-off region

When the voltage of the emitting junction is low than the dead region voltage or equal to zero, $i_B = 0$ and $i_C = 0$. Looking from the characteristic curves the region below the $i_B = 0$ is called cut-off region.

2.2 Low-frequency Amplifiers

2.2.1 DC Biasing Circuits

Figure 2.2.1 shows the basic circuit of common emitter amplifier. The function of the elements in the figure is as follows:

1. Transistor T

It is the amplifying element in the circuit. If there is a weak signal v_i, the distance between the base and the emitter will cause a weak alternating voltage v_{BE} and the base cause a weak alternating current i_B. Owing to the current amplifying function of a transistor, the collector loop will cause a large collector current $i_C = \beta i_B$. From this, it is known that transistor takes controlling function in the circuit. It makes the collector current change correspondingly with the weak base current.

2.R_C

The collector current i_C after amplification produces a voltage drop in R_C, therefore a alternating voltage v_{CE} appears to be the voltage between the collector and the emitter. Obviously R_C is used to convert current amplifying function of a transistor into voltage amplification, the output voltage is much larger than input voltage.

3.V_{CC}

It supplies the reverse bias to the transistor-collecting junction. It is pointed out that the amplifier converts the small input signal into large output signal through controlling function of transistor. The large energy is supplied by V_{CC}.

4. R_B

When V_{CC} is unaltered, through adjusting base bias resistor R_B, it can adjust quiescent operating point of amplifier so that the amplifier has a good operation performance.

5.C_1 & C_2

Because capacitance is infinite large to DC resistance, but drops as rise of current frequency to AC resistance. Therefore the capacitor takes the function of separating DC & conducting AC in the circuit. Obviously C_1 is to send AC signals, which need to be amplified to base and separate DC component so as to guarantee that operating condition of the transistor is not affected by the signal source DC component. C_2 is to send AC voltage after amplification into load and separate DC component. Therefore, C_1 and C_2 are called coupling capacitor.

If we assume $V_{BE(on)} = 0.7\text{V}$, then from Figure 2.2.1 we can see the bias relationship:

$$I_B = \frac{V_{CC} - 0.7}{R_b} \quad (2.2.1)$$

$$I_C = \beta I_B \quad (2.2.2)$$

$$V_{CE} = V_{CC} - I_C R_C \quad (2.2.3)$$

Both V_{CC} and β must be known. I_B, I_C and V_{CE} are called quiescent point. The purpose of setting operating point is to increase base and collector voltage & current of transistor and to avoid dead region so as to make transistor work in a straight period in the characteristic curve. In this way, the output signal has have no distortion.

Chapter 2 Amplifiers

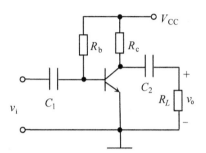

Figure 2.2.1 Basic Circuit of CE Amplifier

The circuit of Figure 2.2.1 is known as a fixed-bias circuit because I_B is fixed mostly by the values of V_{CC} and R_b, which are external to the transistor. The advantage of the circuit is simple. But the disadvantage is that the quiescent operating point is not stable. When the temperature increases, the parameters of transistor such as β, $V_{BE(on)}$ change. The changing results in increasing of I_C, i.e. the quiescent operating point drift. This is not what we want to get.

The most widely used biasing circuit is shown in Figure 2.2.2. Firstly we calculate its quiescent operating point.

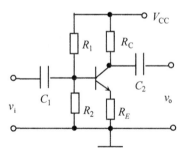

Figure 2.2.2 Stabilized Bias Circuit

We assume $I_1 \gg I_B$, so

$$V_B = \frac{R_2}{R_1 + R_2} V_{CC} \tag{2.2.4}$$

$$V_E = V_B - 0.7$$

$$I_C = \frac{V_E}{R_E}, \quad I_B = \frac{I_C}{\beta}$$
$$V_{CE} = V_{CC} - I_C(R_C + R_E) \tag{2.2.5}$$

Here, R_E provides negative DC feedback; that is the voltage drop across R_E, which has the opposite polarity to the base supply voltage. For example, if the collector current should increase as a result of temperature increase, that is, the voltage drop across R_E will increase, and this in turn results in a decrease in I_B, which tends to offset the original increase in I_C. The process can be written as:

$$T\uparrow \rightarrow I_C\uparrow \rightarrow V_E(=I_C R_E)\uparrow \rightarrow V_{BE}(=V_B-V_E)\rightarrow I_B\downarrow \rightarrow I_C\downarrow$$

which shows the quiescent operating point is stable.

2.2.2 Analyzing Methods of Amplifiers

There are two methods to analyze amplifier. i. e. graphical method and equivalent circuit method. Graphical method is usually used to analyze the DC quiescent point (defined by I_C, I_B, V_{CE}) whether proper and the possible type of distortion in output signals. This method is simple and clear but the error is large. The equivalent circuit method is usually used to analyze AC parameters of amplifier such as voltage gain, input resistor and output resistor.

1. Graphical Method

When we have input and output characteristic curves of a triode and its amplifying circuit as shown in Figure 2.2.1, we can define quiescent point using Graphical method. The steps are as follows:

(1) Obtain I_B from the input loop of an amplifier. In Figure 2.2.1,
$$I_{BQ} = \frac{V_{CC} - 0.7}{R_b}$$

(2) Draw out and determine quiescent point, in output characteristic curves.

From output loop of an amplifier, we can obtain $V_{CE} = V_{CC} - I_C R_C$. When $I_C = 0$, $V_{CE} = V_{CC}$. When $V_{CE} = 0$, $I_C = V_{CC}/R_C$. So in output characteristic curves linking two points A $(0, V_{CC}/R_C)$ and B $(V_{CC}, 0)$, we can obtain the DC load line AB. The slope of AB is $-1/R_C$. The quiescent point of amplifier is both on output characteristic curve $I_B = I_{BQ}$ and the straight line AB. It is seen from Figure 2.2.3 that the point Q can meet the above-mentioned condition. Therefore the point Q is the quiescent point.

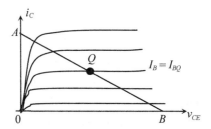

Figure 2.2.3   DC Load Line and Quiescent Point

Usually we desire the point Q is in the middle of AB. In this case, the output signal changing range is large. The voltage gain will be high. If the point Q is selected too low or too high, i_C & v_{CE} will be cut by half waveform shown as Figure 2.2.4. Cut off distortion will be generated if it is too low and saturation distortion will be generated if it is too high.

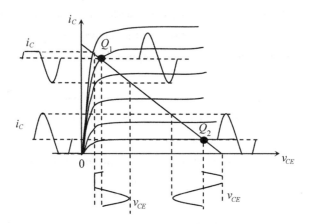

Figure 2.2.4   Distortions due to Improper Quiescent Point

When the point Q is improper, we can adjust the circuit parameter such as R_b, R_C and V_{CC} in order to avoid distortion. Influences of circuit parameters on amplifier's working performance are as follows:

1) R_b

Under the case that the other condition (R_C and V_{CC}) has not changed, R_b is increased and I_B is reduced. Because DC load line is not changed, the new point Q_1 will shift downward and along DC load line as shown in Figure 2.2.5 (a).

2) R_C

The point Q will be changed if R_C changes. If R_C becomes smaller, the slope of DC load line is increased. Therefore, the voltage amplification multiples will be somewhat reduced. If RC is increased much, Q will be shifted to Q_2. The amplifier will enter saturation region and lose its amplifying function.

3) V_{CC}

Under the case that the other condition (R_b and R_C) has not changed, DC load line will be shifted towards right if V_{CC} is increased and its slope has not changed. Due to increase in $I_B = V_{CC}/R_b$, operating point Q will be shifted to Q_1 as shown in Figure 2.2.5 (c). It is known from the diagram that after increase in V_{CC}, it is beneficial to extend changing scope of v_{CE} and reduce distortion. But the power consumed by the amplified circuit is increased. The voltage across the transistor is increased.

In conclusion, changing R_b, R_C and V_{CC} can change quiescent operating point of the amplifier. But it is the most convenient way to adjust quiescent operating point by changing R_b. So in adjusting quiescent operating point, R_b is firstly adjusted.

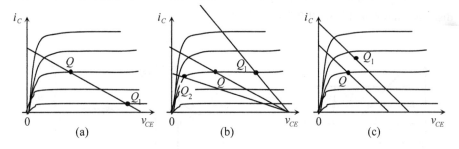

Figure 2.2.5 Influences of Circuit Parameters on the Position Quiescent Operating Point

2. Equivalent Circuit Method

The input and output characteristic curves of a transistor are non-linear, so it is a non-linear element. Transistor amplifying circuit generally belongs to non-linear circuit. Nevertheless if there is a little input signal in the input loop of transistor, it only takes a little change near quiescent operating point, i.e. within a short period in the input characteristic curves as shown in Figure 2.2.6 (a). Therefore this period of curves can be regarded as a straight line. In this case, transistor input loop can be replaced by an equivalent resistor r_{be} as shown in Figure 2.2.6 (b).

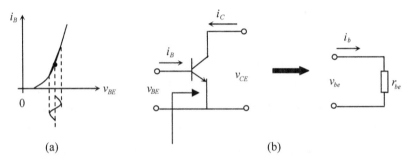

Figure 2.2.6 Input Equivalent Circuit

$$r_{be} = 300 + (1+\beta)\frac{26(\text{mV})}{I_{CQ}(\text{mA})} \qquad (2.2.6)$$

When there is a little input signal in the input loop, the output characteristic curves can be regarded as a group of level line which are parallel and have equal distance shown in Figure 2.2.7.

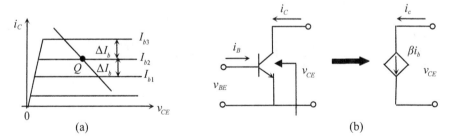

Figure 2.2.7 Output Equivalent Circuit

In conclusion, when transistors work under small signal, its input loop can be replaced by a linear equivalent resistor and its output loop can be indicated by constant current source controlled by I_b, so the transistor can be replaced by an equivalent circuit as shown in Figure 2.2.8. It is pointed out that the equivalent means the changing component of input and output loop. It cannot be used to determine the quiescent operating point of amplifier.

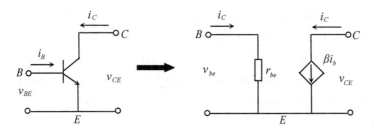

Figure 2.2.8　Simplified the Equivalent Circuit of a Triode

2.2.3　Common-Emitters

Once the Q-point has been established by a biasing circuit, an input voltage can be across the coupling capacitors, as shown in Figure 2.2.9. C_1 and C_2 isolate the dc signal biasing circuit from the input signal v_S and the load resistance R_L, respectively. If the input signal v_S was connected directly to the base without C_1.

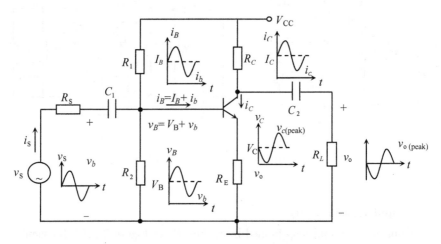

Figure 2.2.9　CE Amplifier Circuit

The source resistance R_S would be form a parallel circuit with R_2 and the base potential V_B would be disturbed. Similarly, the collector potential V_C would depend on R_L if C_2 was removed.

Let us assume that the capacitors have large values so that they are virtually short-circuited at the frequency of the input signal v_S. With a sinusoidal input voltage $v_S = V_m \sin\omega t$, the base potential will be $v_B = V_B + v_b$. If the base current i_B swings between $I_B + i_{b(\text{peak})}$ and $I_B - i_{b(\text{peak})}$, the collector current i_C will swing between $I_C + i_{c(\text{peak})}$ and $I_C - i_{c(\text{peak})}$. The voltage v_{CE} vary from $V_C - R_C(I_c + i_{c(\text{peak})})$ to $V_C - R_C(I_c - i_{c(\text{peak})})$. These waveforms are depicted in Figure 2.2.9. Since C_2 will block any dc signal, the output voltage will vary from $-(R_C /\!/ R_L) i_{c(\text{max})}$ to $(R_C /\!/ R_L) i_{c(\text{min})}$.

1. AC Equivalent Circuit

Since a DC supply offer zero resistance to an AC signal, V_{CC} can be short-circuited. That is, one side of both R_1 and R_C is connected to the ground. The AC equivalent circuit of the amplifier in Figure 2.2.9 is shown in Figure 2.2.10(a), in which V_{CC}, C_1 and C_2 are short-circuited. Replacing the transistor with its model in Figure 2.2.8 gives the small-signal AC equivalent circuit, which can be represented by the equivalent voltage amplifier shown in Figure 2.2.10(b).

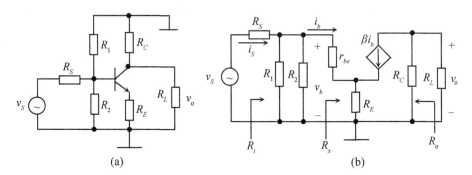

Figure 2.2.10 Equivalent Circuits of CE Amplifier

2. Input Resistance R_i

Using KVL around loop formed by r_{be} and R_E in Figure 2.2.10(b) yields

$$v_b = r_{be} + i_e R_E = i_b [\, r_{be} + (1+\beta) R_E \,] \qquad (2.2.7)$$

Which gives the resistance R_x at the base of the resistor as

$$R_x = \frac{v_b}{i_b} = r_{be} + (1+\beta) R_E \qquad (2.2.8)$$

Thus, the input resistance of the amplifier is the parallel combination of R_1, R_2 and R_x, that is

$$R_i = \frac{v_b}{i_S} = R_1 // R_2 // R_x \qquad (2.2.9)$$

3. Output Resistance R_o

Output resistance R_o, Thevenin's resistance, can be calculated from Figure 2.2.10(b) if v_S is short-circuited and a test voltage v_x is applied across R_C. Since $v_S = 0$, the dependent source current will be zero—that is, the circuit will be open-circuited. The output resistance will simply be R_C. That is

$$R_o = R_C \qquad (2.2.10)$$

4. Voltage Gain A_V

$$v_o = -i_C (R_C // R_L) = -\beta i_b (R_C // R_L) \qquad (2.2.11)$$

$$v_b = r_{be} + i_e R_E = i_b [\, r_{be} + (1+\beta) R_E \,] \qquad (2.2.12)$$

$$A_V = \frac{v_o}{v_i} = -\beta \frac{R_C // R_L}{r_{be} + (1+\beta) R_E} \qquad (2.2.13)$$

This equation indicates that the voltage gain A_V can be made large (a) by letting $R_E = 0$, (b) by using a transistor with a large value of g_m (or β), and (c) by choosing a high value of R_C. Letting $R_E = 0$ will decrease the input resistance R_x and the amplifier will get more current from the input source, but the dc biasing point also depends on R_C and R_E. These conflicting constraints—a higher value of R_E for a larger input resistance and a lower value for a larger voltage gain—can be satisfied by using two emitter resistors R_{E1} and R_{E2}, as shown in Figure 2.2.11. R_{E11} and R_{E2} set the DC biasing point, and R_{E1} gives the desired AC input resistance or voltage gain. The analysis of this circuit is similar to the derivations above, except that R_{E1} is used instead of R_E. For DC biasing calculations, however, $R_E (= R_{E1} + R_{E2})$ should be used. It is often necessary to compromise among the design specifications for the biasing point, the input resistance, and the voltage gain. It is not always possible to satisfy all the design specifications.

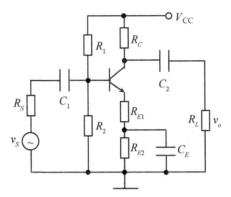

Figure 2.2.11 Another CE Amplifier

2.2.4 Emitter Followers

A common-collector amplifier is generally known as an emitter follower, because the emitter voltage follows the voltage at the base terminal. Such an amplifier has a low output resistance and a high input resistance. It is commonly used as a buffer stage between a load and the source. This arrangement is shown in Figure 2.2.12(a), in which R_B sets the biasing base current. The equivalent circuit for DC analysis is shown in Figure 2.2.12(b). Replacing the transistor with its model in Figure 2.2.8, gives the small-signal AC equivalent circuit shown in Figure 2.2.12(c). We need to determine the Q-point before we can find the small-signal transistor parameter. Using KVL around the loop formed by V_{CC}, R_B, V_{BE}, and R_E in Figure 2.2.12 (b), we get

$$V_{CC} = R_B I_B + V_{BE} + R_E I_E = R_B I_B + V_{BE} + R_E(1+\beta) I_B \quad (2.2.14)$$

which gives the biasing base current I_B as

$$I_B = \frac{V_{CC} - V_{BE}}{R_B + (1+\beta) R_E} \quad (2.2.15)$$

from which we can find $I_C = \beta I_B$. Then V_{CE} is given by

$$V_{CE} = V_{CC} - R_E I_E = V_{CC} - R_E(1+\beta) I_B \quad (2.2.16)$$

1. Input Resistance R_i

When the load resistance R_L is connected to the amplifier, R_L becomes parallel to R_E and will affect the input resistance. Unlike the case of a CE amplifier, in an emitter follower R_L should be included in finding the input resistance R_i. Using KVL around the base-emitter loop in Figure 2.2.12(c), we get

$$v_b = i_b r_{be} + i_e (R_E // R_L) = i_b [r_{be} + (1+\beta)(R_E // R_L)] \qquad (2.2.17)$$

which gives the resistance R_x at the base of the transistor as

$$R_x = \frac{v_b}{i_b} = r_{be} + (1+\beta)(R_E // R_L) \qquad (2.2.18)$$

$$R_i = R_x // R_B \qquad (2.2.19)$$

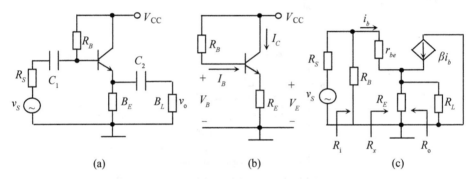

Figure 2.2.12 Emitter Follower

2. Voltage Gain A_V

$$v_o = i_e (R_E // R_L) = (1+\beta) i_b (R_E // R_L) \qquad (2.2.20)$$

$$v_b = r_{be} + i_e R_E = i_b [r_{be} + (1+\beta)(R_E // R_L)] \qquad (2.2.21)$$

$$A_V = \frac{v_o}{v_i} = \frac{(1+\beta)(R_E // R_L)}{r_{be} + (1+\beta)(R_E // R_L)} \qquad (2.2.22)$$

For $r_{be} \ll (1+\beta) R_E // R_L$, $A_V \approx 1$.

3. Output Resistance R_o

Output resistance R_o can be calculated by applying a test voltage v_x across the output terminals and letting the input v_S short-circuited, as shown in Figure 2.2.13. The base current i_b flows through r_{be}, which is in series with the parallel combination of R_S and R_B, so

$$i_b = \frac{-v_x}{r_{be} + (R_S // R_B)}$$

Using Kirchhoff's current law (KCL) at the emitter junction yields

$$i_x = \frac{v_x}{R_E} - \beta i_b - i_b = v_x \left[\frac{1}{R_E} + \frac{1+\beta}{r_{be}+R_S /\!/ R_B} \right] \qquad (2.2.23)$$

which gives the output resistance R_o as

$$R_o = \frac{v_x}{i_x} = R_E /\!/ \frac{r_{be}+R_S /\!/ R_B}{1+\beta} \qquad (2.2.24)$$

thus, R_o is the parallel combination of R_E and $[r_{be}+(R_S /\!/ R_B)]$ reflected from the i_b branch into the i_e branch. Since $\beta \gg 1$ and $R_S \ll R_B$, the output resistance R_o can be approximated by $R_o \approx \frac{r_{be}+R_S}{\beta}$.

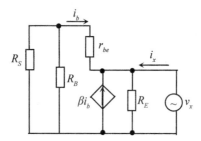

Figure 2.2.13 Equivalent Circuit for Determining R_o

2.3 Field-Effect Transistors

Field-effect transistors (FETs) are the next generation of transistor after BJTs. A BJT current-controlled device, and its output current depends on the base current. The input resistance of a BJT is inversely proportional to the collector current ($25.8\text{mV}/I_C$), and it is low. The current in BJTs depends on both the majority and the minority of carriers. The current in FETs, on the other hand, depends on only one type of carrier: the majority of carriers (either electrons or holes). The output current of an FET is controlled by an electric field that depends on a controlled voltage. An FET is a unipolar device and used as a voltage-controlled device.

The basic concept of FETs has been known since the 1930s; however, FETs did not find practical applications until the early 1960s. Since the late 1970s, MOSFETs have become very popular; they are increasingly being used in integrated circuits (ICs). The manufacture of MOSFETs is relatively simple compared to that of bipolar transistors. A MOSFET device can be made small, and it occupies a small silicon area in an IC chip. MOSFETs are currently used for very-large-scale integrated (VLSI) circuits such as microprocessors and memory chips.

There are three types of FETs: enhancement metal-oxide field-effect transistors, depletion metal-oxide field-effect transistors (both of which are known as MOSFETs), and junction field-effect transistors (JFETs). Each type can be either n-channel or p-channel. An FET has three terminals: the drain (D), the gate (G), and the source (S). The symbols for FETs are shown in Figure 2.3.1.

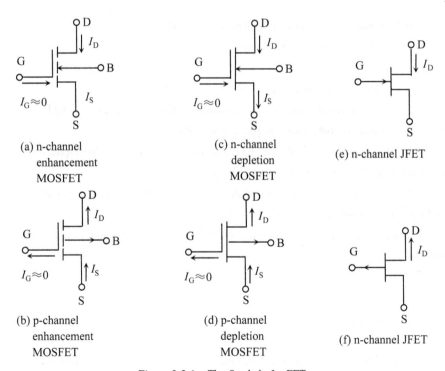

Figure 2.3.1 The Symbols for FETs

An FET is a voltage-controlled nonlinear device. A voltage between the gate and the source develops an electric field, which then controls the flow of drain current. Therefore, the drain current depends on the gate-source voltage, and an FET has amplifying function.

The output characteristic of an FET can be divided into three regions: the cutoff region, in which the FET is in the off state; the saturation region, in which the transistor exhibits a high output resistance and has amplifying function; and the ohmic region, in which the transistor offers a low resistance. An FET is used as an amplifier in the saturation region and as a switch in the ohmic region.

An FET should be biased properly in order to activate the device and also to establish a DC operating point such that a small variation in the gate-source voltage causes a variation in the drain current. Like a BJT amplifier, an FET amplifier can be used as a buffer stage to offer a low output resistance and a high input resistance.

An FET has the following advantages over a BJT:

(1) It has an extremely high input resistance, on the order of megaohms.

(2) It has no offset voltage when it is used as a switch, whereas a BJT requires a minimum base-emitter voltage V_{BE}.

(3) It is relatively immune to ionizing radiation, whereas a BJT is very sensitive because its beta value is particularly affected.

(4) It is less "noisy" than a BJT and thus more suitable for input stages of low-level amplifier. It is used extensively in FM receivers.

(5) It provides better thermal stability than a BJT-that is, the parameters of FETs are less sensitive to temperature changes.

FETs have a smaller gain bandwidth than BJTs and the more susceptible to damage in handling. The gain bandwidth is the frequency at which the gain becomes unity.

2.4 Cascaded Amplifiers

An amplifier operates at a dc Q-point and is subjected to two types of signals: AC signals and DC signals. Often, several amplifiers are cascaded by coupling capacitors, as shown in Figure 2.4.1, so that the AC signal from the source can flow from one stage to the next stage while the DC signal is blocked. As a result, the DC biasing voltages of the amplifiers do not affect the signal source, adjacent stages, or the load. Such cascaded amplifiers are called capacitive (or AC) coupled amplifiers. However, amplifiers in integrated circuits are connected directly, because capacitors cannot be fabricated in an integrated form; such amplifiers are called direct (or DC) coupled amplifiers.

After the capacitor coupling is adopted, not only the AC signal of the front stage can be transferred to the next stage smoothly but also the front and rear quiescent operating points can be protected from mutual influence.

Figure 2.4.1 shows the RC coupled two-stage voltage amplifier. As the basic principle of the single-stage amplifier in the figure and the functions of each element are same as before.

C_2 is a coupling capacitor. It can isolate the DC voltages of the front and rear stage and send the amplified AC signal in the first stage to the second stage for further amplification.

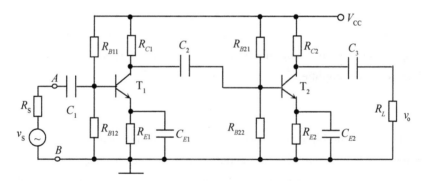

Figure 2.4.1 RC Coupled Two-stage Voltage Amplifier

In order to further find out the mutual influence between stages of multi-stage amplifier and between the same signal source of the amplifier and the load resistance. The concepts of the input and output resistances of the amplifier are discussed as follows

2.4.1 Input Resistance

A transistor amplifier always gets current from the signal source or from the front stage amplifier. Therefore an amplifier is connected to the signal source, it is equal to a load resistance of the signal source. This load resistance of the signal source is the input resistance of the amplifier. Thus it is seen that the input resistance of amplifier is the resistance, which is seen from the terminals A-B in Figure 2.4.2. In the figure, v_S is the electromotive force of signal source, and R_S is the inner resistance of the signal source. The circuit in the block is the equivalent circuit of the amplifier as shown in Figure 2.4.2.

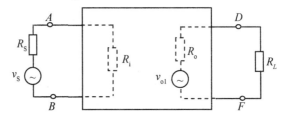

Figure 2.4.2　The Circuit for Analyzing

When the variation of the input voltage is equal to v_i, the current variation of the input circuit of the amplifier is i_i and the ratio of v_i to i_i is just the input resistance of the amplifier.

$$R_i = \frac{v_i}{i_i} \qquad (2.4.1)$$

The higher the input resistance is the lower the current from the signal source (or from the front stage) by the amplifier may be. So the magnitude of Ri will directly affect the operating states of the signal source or the front-stage amplifier.

Power V_{CC} and capacitances are equivalent to short-circuit. So the AC channel of the amplifier can be sketched as shown in Figure 2.4.3.

From Figure 2.4.3, $R_i = R_{B11} // R_{B12} // r_{be}$.

2.4.2　Output Resistance

After the output terminal of the amplifier is terminated by a load. The output voltage v_o of the amplifier will be less than that without load. From the terminals D-F of the amplifier, the whole amplifier looks like an equivalent power, which is controlled by an input signal as shown in Figure 2.4.3. The inner resistance of the equivalent power is the output resistance of the amplifier. From Figure 2.4.3, $R_o = R_{C2}$.

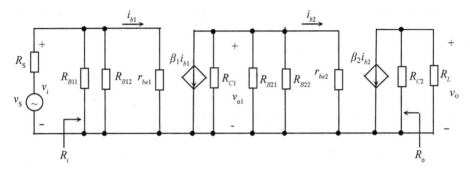

Figure 2.4.3 The AC Channel of the Amplifier

As R_{C2} is usually thousands of ohms, the output resistance of the common emitter amplifier is higher.

For a multi-stage amplifier, it is always required that the resistance of the input stage be higher so as to get less current from the signal source. It is also required that the resistance of the output stage be lower so as to drive more load.

2.4.3 Voltage Gain of the Multi-stage Amplifier

Since the output voltage v_{o1} of the front stage of the multi-stage amplifier is just the input voltage v_{i2} of the rear stage. Its voltage amplification is

$$A_V = \frac{v_o}{v_i} = \frac{v_{o1}}{v_i} \frac{v_o}{v_{o1}} = A_{V1} A_{V2} = -\frac{\beta_1(R_{C1} // R_{i2})}{r_{be1}} \times \left[-\frac{\beta_2(R_{C2} // R_L)}{r_{be2}} \right] \quad (2.4.2)$$

The input resistance of the rear stage $R_{i2} = R_{B21} // R_{B22} // r_{be}$, it is the load of the front stage.

It is therefore obvious that the general voltage amplification of multi-stage amplifier is equal to the product of the voltage amplification of each stage.

It should be pointed out that the above-mentioned voltage amplification of each stage has already considered the input resistance of the rear stage as the load of the front stage. Therefore its amplification is lower as compared with that without load of each stage

2.4.4 Frequency Response of the RC-coupled Amplifier

So far, we have assumed that there are no reactive elements in an amplifier and that the gain of an amplifier remains constant at all frequencies. However, the gain of practical amplifiers is frequency-dependent, and even the input and output resistances of amplifiers vary with the frequency.

Usually the input signal of amplifier is not sine wave with a single frequency, but the total sine wave with different frequency components. For example, when the human's language or music is transferred to an electric signal, the signal frequency range is usually several hertz to ten thousand hertz. This is so called audio range. In fact, it impossible for an ideal amplifier to employ the same amplifies ability for all frequencies. It takes a certain time for the carrier (electron or hole) to be transmitted to the collector area. The carrier filled to the base region will not reach to the collector entirely when the signal frequency is high. At this time, the input signal changes its polarity quickly. Thus the collector current will reduce the varying amplitude within the positive and negative half circles. Otherwise it will decrease the current gain of transistor. Therefore the voltage gain will drop and rise according to the frequency variation when it is at high frequency. On the other hand, when the signal frequency is very low, since the capacitive resistance of the coupling capacitance and bypass capacitance of the emitter is increased, the amplification of the amplifier will also decreased with the decrement of the frequency. In order to reduce the loss of the low-frequency signal in the coupling-capacitance, big coupled-capacitances (about 10-50 microfarads) are usually used in the low-frequency amplifier. Generally speaking, the magnitude of the coupled-capacitance can't be calculated accurately.

The relation between A_V of amplifier and the frequency f is called amplifier frequency response, as shown in Figure 2.4.4.

In a range of low frequency and high frequency, when the voltage gain A_V drops to 0.707 times the voltage gain A_{V_0} in the intermediate frequency range, the frequency now is called lower cut-off frequency f_L and upper cut-off frequency f_H. The frequency range between $f_H - f_L$ is called pass band of the amplifier.

For AC amplifier used in the control system, the smooth frequency characteristics is required in the required bandwidth.

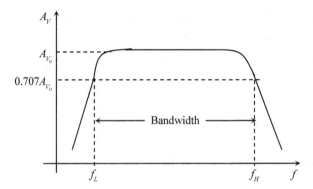

Figure 2.4.4　Frequency Response of Amplifier

2.5　Active Sources and Differential Amplifiers

Differential amplifiers are commonly used as an input stage in various types of analog ICs, such as operational amplifiers, voltage comparators, voltage regulators, video amplifiers, power amplifiers, and balanced modulators and demodulators. A differential amplifier is a very important transistor stage and determines many of the performance characteristics of an IC. In ICs, including differential amplifiers, it is unnecessary to bias transistors by setting the values of biasing resistors. Because of variations in resistor values, power supply, and temperature, the quiescent point of transistors changes. Transistors can be used to generate the characteristics of dc sources. Transistors can also be used to produce an output voltage source that is independent of its load or equivalently, of the output current.

2.5.1　Internal Structure of Differential Amplifiers

A differential amplifier acts as an input stage: its output voltage is proportional to the difference between its two input voltages v_{B1} and v_{B2}. An op-amp with a differential stage is shown in Figure 2.5.1(a). It has a high voltage gain and is directly dc-coupled to the input voltages and the load. As we will see later in this chapter, the voltage gain of a differential amplifier depends directly on the output resistance of the current source acting as an active load.

In amplifiers with discrete components, passive components such as resistors and capacitors are less expensive than active devices such as transistors; thus, in multistage amplifiers, interstage coupling is accomplished with capacitors. However, in monolithic circuits, die area is the principal factor for determining cost. Capacitors with the values and sizes used in amplifiers made with discrete components cannot be included in ICs and must be external to the chip. But using external capacitors increases the pin count of the package and the cost of the ICs. In order to eliminate capacitors, a dc-coupled circuit is used. The cheapest component in an integrated circuit is the one that can be fabricated within the least area, usually the transistor. The optimal integrated circuit has as less resistors and more transistors as possible.

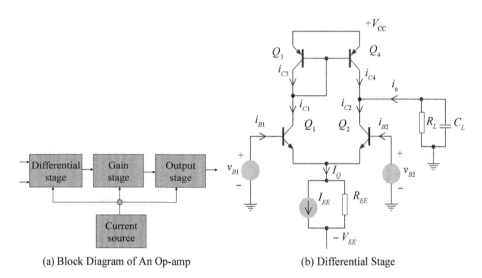

(a) Block Diagram of An Op-amp (b) Differential Stage

Figure 2.5.1 Typical Differential Amplifier

A differential amplifier can serve as a direct dc-coupled differential stage. A typical amplifier, as shown in Figure 2.5.1(b), can be divided into four parts: (1) a dc-biasing constant current source, represented by I_Q and R_{EE}; (2) an active load, consisting of transistors Q_3 and Q_4; (3) a load, represented by R_L and C_L for the next stage; and (4) a direct-coupled differential pair, consisting of transistors Q_1 and Q_2.

2.5.2 BJT Current Sources

Transistor current sources are widely used in analog integrated circuits, both as biasing elements and as loads for amplifying stages. Transistor current sources are less sensitive than resistors to variations in dc power supply and temperature. Especially for small values of biasing current, transistor current sources are more economical than resistors because of the greater die area required for resistors.

The current in Figure 2.5.1(b) enter the current source circuit; this type of constant current source is often referred to as a current sink. In contrast, the current of the active load consisting of transistors Q_3 and Q_4 flows out of the current source circuit; this type of constant current source is referred to as a current source. Therefore, a constant current source can behave as either a current source of a current sink. An ideal current source should maintain a constant current with an infinite output resistance under all operating conditions. The most commonly used current sources are the basic current source, the modified basic current source, the Widlar current source, the Cascode current source, and the Wilson current source.

1. Basic Current Source

The simplest current source consists of a resistor and two transistors, as shown in Figure 2.5.2. Transistor Q_1 is diode-connected, and its collector-base voltage is forced to zero: $v_{CB}=0$. Thus, the collector-base junction is off, and Q_1 will operate in the active region. Transistor Q_2 can be in the active region as well as in the saturation region.

Let us assume that Q_1 and Q_2 are identical transistors whose leakage currents are negligible and whose output resistances are infinite. Since the two transistors have the same base-emitter voltages (that is, $V_{BE1}=V_{BE2}$), the collector and base currents are equal: $I_{C1}=I_{C2}$ and $I_{B1}=I_{B2}$. Applying Kirchhoff's current law (KCL) at the collector of Q_1 gives the reference current:

$$I_R = I_{C1} + I_{B1} + I_{B2} = I_{C1} + 2I_{B1}$$

Since $I_{C1}=\beta_F I_{B1}$,

$$I_R = I_{C1} + 2I_{B1} = I_{C1} + 2I_{C1}/\beta_F$$

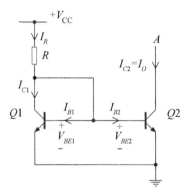

Figure 2.5.2 Basic Current Source

which gives the collector current I_{C1} as

$$I_{C1} = I_{C2} = \frac{I_R}{1 + \frac{2}{\beta_F}} \quad (2.5.1)$$

$$= \frac{V_{CC} - V_{BE1}}{R_1} \times \frac{1}{1 + \frac{2}{\beta_F}} \quad (2.5.2)$$

If the dc current gain $\beta_F \gg 2$, which is usually the case, Equation (2.5.2) is reduced to

$$I_{C1} = I_{C2} \approx I_R$$

Thus, for two identical transistors, the reference and output currents are almost equal. I_{C2} which is the mirror image of I_{C1}, is know as the mirror current of I_{C1}. For transistors with small values of β_F, the current ratio will not be unity. In practice, however, the transistors may not identical and the two collector currents will have a constant ratio.

2.Modified Basic Current Source

Notice from Equation (2.5.1) that the collector current $I_{C2}(=I_{C1})$ differs from the reference current I_R by a factor of $(1 + 2/\beta_F)$. For low-gain transistors (especially pnp types), I_{C2} and I_R can not be concidered approximately equal. The error can be reduced by adding another transistor so that I_{C2} becomes less dependent on the transistor parameter β_F. This type of circuit is shown in Figure 2.5.3. Appling KCL at the emitter of transistor Q_3 gives

$$I_{E3} = I_{B1} + I_{B2} = \frac{I_{C1}}{\beta_F} + \frac{I_{C2}}{\beta_F} \qquad (2.5.3)$$

Since $V_{BE1} = V_{BE2}$, it follows that $I_{C1} = I_{C2}$. Thus, Equation (2.5.3) becomes

$$I_{E3} = \frac{2}{\beta_F} I_{C2}$$

The base current of Q_3 is related to I_{E3} by

$$I_{B3} = \frac{I_{E3}}{1+\beta_F} = \frac{2}{\beta_F(1+\beta_F)} I_{C2} \qquad (2.5.4)$$

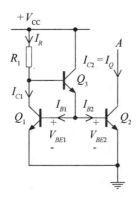

Figure 2.5.3 Modified Basic Source

Using KCL at the collector of Q_1 gives

$$I_R = I_{C1} + I_{B3} = I_{C1} + \frac{2}{\beta_F(1+\beta_F)} I_{C2} \qquad (2.5.5)$$

Since $I_{C1} = I_{C2}$, Equation (2.5.5) gives the output current I_0 as

$$I_0 = I_{C2} = \frac{I_R}{1 + \dfrac{2}{\beta_F^2 + \beta_F}} \qquad (2.5.6)$$

which indicates that the reference current I_R is related to the output current I_0 by a factor of only $1 + \dfrac{2}{\beta_F^2 + \beta_F}$. The reference current can be found from

$$I_R = \frac{V_{CC} - V_{BE1} - V_{BE3}}{R_1} \qquad (2.5.7)$$

In the derivation of Equation (2.5.6), the output resistances of the transistors are neglected.

3. Widlar Current Source

Biasing currents of low magnitudes, typically on the order of 5μA, are required in a variety of application. Currents of low magnitude can be obtained by inserting a resistance of moderate value in series with the emitter Q_2 in Figure 2.5.2. A circuit with this modification, as shown in Figure 2.5.4, is known as a Widlar current source. As a result of the addition of R_2 to the circuit, I_{C2} is no longer equal to I_R, and the value of I_{C2} can be made much smaller than that of I_{C1}. This circuit can give currents in the μA range, with acceptable circuit resistance values of less than 50kΩ.

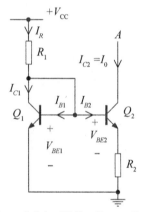

Figure 2.5.4 Widlar Current Source

Using KVL around the base-emitter loop in Figure 2.5.4 gives
$$V_{BE1} - V_{BE2} - (I_{C2} + I_{B2}) R_2 = 0$$
Since $I_{C2} \gg I_{B2}$,
$$V_{BE1} - V_{BE2} - I_{C2} R_2 \left(1 + \frac{1}{\beta_F}\right) = 0 \qquad (2.5.8)$$
The reference current I_R can be found from
$$I_R = \frac{V_{CC} - V_{BE1}}{R_1} \qquad (2.5.9)$$
which is also related to the base and collector currents. That is,
$$I_R = I_{C1} + I_{B1} + I_{B2} = I_{C1}\left(1 + \frac{1}{\beta_F}\right) + \frac{I_{C2}}{\beta_F} \qquad (2.5.10)$$

2.5 Active Sources and Differential Amplifiers 65

4. Cascode Current Source

The emitter resistance R_2 in the Widlar current can be replaced by a basic current source consisting of two transistor Q_3 and Q_4. This arrangement shown in Figure 2.5.5 will give a large output resistance. In a cascode-like connection, two or more transistors are connected in series so that their collector biasing currents are almost identical, whereas in a cascode-like connection, the transistors operate in parallel fashion so that one transistor drives the other. The larger the output resistance, the greater the voltage gain of an amplifier.

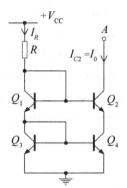

Figure 2.5.5 Cascode Current Source

5. Wilson Current Source

A Wilson current source, as shown in Figure 2.5.6, also gives a high output

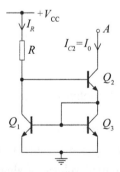

Figure 2.5.6 Wilson Current Source

resistance. However, the output current is approximately equal to the reference current. $I_O = I_R$

6. Multiple Current Source

A dc reference current can be generated in one location and reproduced in another location for biasing amplifier circuits in ICs. A group of current sources with only one reference current is shown in Figure 2.5.7. This is an extension of the modified basic current source. The transistor Q_1 and the resistor R_1 serve as the reference for current-sink the transistors Q_3 through Q_6. The transistor Q_2 supplies the total base currents for the transistors and makes the collector current of Q_1 almost equal to the reference current I_R. That is, $I_R \approx I_{C1}$. The collector currents I_1 and I_2 will be mirrors of current I_R. I_3 will be the two times I_R, because Q_5 and Q_6 are the parallel combination. Q_5 and Q_6 should be equivalent to a single transistor whose emitter-base junction has double the area of Q_1. Therefore, the emitter areas of transistors can be scaled in ICs so as to provide multiples of the reference current simply by designing the transistors so that they have an area ratio equal to the desired multiple.

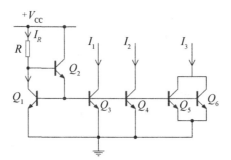

Figure 2.5.7 Multiple Current Sources

2.5.3 Characteristics of Differential Amplifiers

The differential stage in Figure 2.5.1 can be represented by an equivalent amplifier, as shown in Figure 2.5.8. If the two input voltages are equal, a differential amplifier gives an output voltage of almost zero. Its voltage gain is very large, so the input voltage is low, typically less than 50mV. Thus, we can consider the input voltages as small signals with zero dc components.

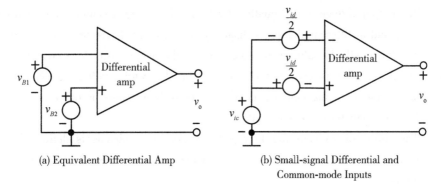

(a) Equivalent Differential Amp

(b) Small-signal Differential and Common-mode Inputs

Figure 2.5.8 Small-signal Equivalent Circuit with Differential and Common-mode Inputs

Let us define a differential voltage v_{id} as

$$v_{id} = v_{i1} - v_{i2} \tag{2.5.11}$$

and a common-mode voltage v_{ic} as

$$v_{ic} = \frac{v_{i1} + v_{i2}}{2} \tag{2.5.12}$$

From Equations (2.5.11) and (2.5.12), the two input voltages can be expressed as

$$v_{i1} = v_{ic} + \frac{v_{id}}{2} \tag{2.5.13}$$

and

$$v_{i2} = v_{ic} - \frac{v_{id}}{2} \tag{2.5.14}$$

By replacing the input signals with the equivalent differential and common-mode signals, we can represent the differential stage by an equivalent amplifier, as shown in Figure 2.5.8(b). Let v_{od} be the output voltage due to v_{id} only, and let v_{oc} be the output voltage due to v_{ic} only. The output voltage of the differential stage can be obtained by applying the superposition theorem. That is

$$v_o = v_{od} + v_{oc} = A_{vd} v_{id} + A_{vc} v_{ic} \tag{2.5.15}$$

where $A_{vd} = \dfrac{v_{od}}{v_{id}} =$ differential voltage gain

$$A_{vd} = \frac{v_{oc}}{v_{ic}} = \text{common-mode voltage gain}$$

The output voltage v_o in Equation (2.5.15) is due to a common-mode input voltage v_{ic} and a differential input voltage v_{id}. If A_{vd} is much greater than A_{vc}, the output voltage will be almost independent of the common-mode signal v_{ic}. A differential amplifier is expected to amplify the differential voltage as much as possible, while rejecting common-mode signals such as noise or other unwanted signal, which will be present in both terminals.

The ability of an amplifier to reject common-mode signals is defined by a performance criterion called the common-mode rejection ratio K_{CMR}, which is defined as

$$K_{CMR} = \left|\frac{A_{vd}}{A_{vc}}\right| = 20\log\left|\frac{A_{vd}}{A_{vc}}\right| \text{ (in dB)} \qquad (2.5.16)$$

which shows that, to reduce the effect of v_{ic} on the output voltage v_o—that is, to get v_{oc} to approach zero—the value of K_{CMR} must be very large, tending to infinity for an ideal amplifier. Thus, a differential amplifier should behave differently for common-mode and differential signals.

2.5.4 Differential Amplifier Circuit

The differential amplifier circuit is an extremely popular connection used in IC units. This connection can be described by considering the basic differential amplifier shown in Figure 2.5.9. Notice that the circuit has two separate inputs and two separate outputs, and that the emitters are connected together. Whereas most differential amplifier circuits use two separate voltage supplies, the circuit can also operate using a single supply.

A number of input signal combinations are possible:

If an input signal is applied to either input with the other input connected to ground, the operation is referred to as "single-ended." If two opposite-polarity input signals are applied, the operation is referred to as "double-ended". If the same input is applied to both inputs, the operation is called "common-mode".

In single-ended operation, a single input signal is applied. However, due to the common-emitter connection, the input signal operates both transistors, resulting in output from both collectors.

2.5 Active Sources and Differential Amplifiers

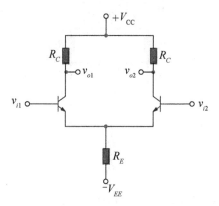

Figure 2.5.9 Basic Differential Amplifier Circuit

In double-ended operation, two input signals are applied, the difference of the inputs resulting in outputs from both collectors due to the difference of the signals applied to both inputs.

In common-mode operation, the common input signal results in opposite signals at each collector, and these signals cancel out so that the resulting output signal is zero. As a practical matter, the opposite signals can not be completely canceled, and a small signal results.

The main feature of the differential amplifier is that it has a very large gain when opposite signals are applied to the inputs as compared to a very small gain resulting from common inputs.

1. DC Bias

Let's first consider the dc bias operation of the circuit of Figure 2.5.9. Inputs signals are obtained from voltage source, so the dc voltage at each input is essentially connected to 0V, as shown in Figure 2.5.10. With each base voltage at 0V, the common-emitter dc bias voltage is

$$V_E = 0 - V_{BE} = -0.7\text{V} \qquad (2.5.17)$$

So the emitter dc bias current is

$$I_E = \frac{V_E - (-V_{EE})}{R_E} \approx \frac{V_{EE} - 0.7\text{V}}{R_E} \qquad (2.5.18)$$

Assuming that the transistors are well matched, we obtain

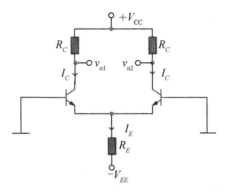

Figure 2.5.10 DC Bias of Differential Amplifier Circuit

$$I_{C1} = I_{C2} = \frac{I_E}{2}$$

resulting in a collector voltage of

$$V_{C1} = V_{C2} = V_{CC} - I_C R_C = V_{CC} - \frac{I_E}{2} R_C \qquad (2.5.19)$$

2. AC Operation of Circuit

An ac connection of a differential amplifier is shown in Figure 2.5.11. Separate input signals are applied as v_{i1} and v_{i2}, we can get two separate outputs as v_{o1} and v_{o2}. For ac analysis, we redraw the circuit in Figure 2.5.12. Each transistor is replaced by its ac equivalent.

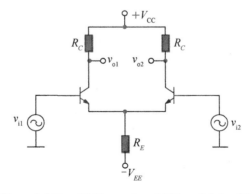

Figure 2.5.11 AC Donnection of Differential Amplifier

2.5 Active Sources and Differential Amplifiers   71

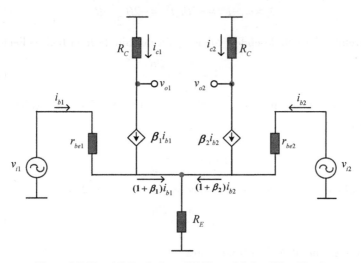

Figure 2.5.12   AC Equivalent of Differential Amplifier Circuit

3. Double-Ended AC Voltage Gain

To calculate the double-ended ac voltage gain, v_o/v_i, apply two opposite-polarity signals to two input terminals separately, as shown in Figure 2.5.11. The ac equivalent circuit is drawn in Figure 2.5.12. If we assumes the two transistors are well matched, then

$$r_{be1} = r_{be2} = r_{be}$$
$$\beta_1 = \beta_2 = \beta$$

Assuming $v_{i1} = -v_{i2}$, the ac base current can be calculated based on the principle of KVL(kirchhoff's voltage law), resulting

$$i_{b1} = -i_{b2} = i_b$$
$$v_{i1} - v_{i2} = 2i_b r_{be}$$

Define the differential input voltage as $v_{id} = v_{i1} - v_{i2}$, then

$$i_b = \frac{v_{id}}{2r_{be}}$$

$$v_{o1} = -i_{c1} R_C = -\beta i_b R_C$$
$$v_{o2} = -i_{c2} R_C = -\beta i_b R_C$$

then the output voltage from the two collectors is

$$v_o = v_{o1} - v_{o2} = -2\beta i_b R_C = -2\beta \frac{v_{id}}{2r_{be}} R_C \qquad (2.5.20)$$

Therefore, the double-ended voltage gain magnitude from both collectors is

$$A_d = \frac{v_o}{v_{id}} = -\frac{\beta R_C}{r_{be}} \qquad (2.5.21)$$

If the output signal is from collector 1, the double-ended voltage gain at collector 1 is

$$A_{v1} = \frac{v_{o1}}{v_{id}} = -\frac{\beta R_C}{2r_{be}} \qquad (2.5.22)$$

For which the double-ended voltage gain at collector 2 is

$$A_{v2} = \frac{v_{o2}}{v_{id}} = \frac{\beta R_C}{2r_{be}} \qquad (2.5.23)$$

4. Single-Ended AC Voltage Gain

To calculate the single-ended ac voltage gain v_o/v_i. v_{i1} is connected to one input with v_{i2} connected to ground, as shown in Figure 2.5.13. The ac equivalent of this connection is drawn in Figure 2.5.14. The ac base current can be calculated using the base 1 input KVL equation. If we assumes that the two transistors are well matched, then

$$i_{b1} = -i_{b1} = i_b$$

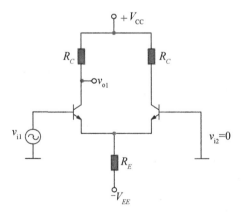

Figure 2.5.13 Single-ended Differential Amplifier Circuit

2.5 Active Sources and Differential Amplifiers

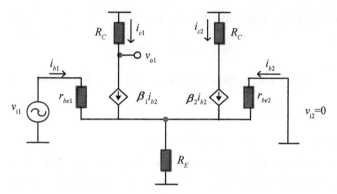

Figure 2.5.14 AC Equivalent of Circuit in Figure 2.5.13

With R_E very large (ideally infinite), the circuit for obtaining the KVL equation simplifies to that of Figure 2.5.15, from which we can write

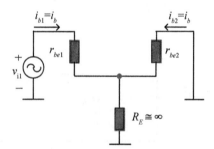

Figure 2.5.15 Partial Circuit for Calculating i_p

$$v_{i1} - i_b r_{be} - i_b r_{be} = 0$$

so that

$$i_b = \frac{v_{i1}}{2r_{be}}$$

If we also assume that

$$\beta_1 = \beta_2 = \beta$$

then

$$i_c = \beta i_b = \beta \frac{v_{i1}}{2r_{be}}$$

and the output voltage magnitude at collector 1 is

$$v_o = v_{o1} = -i_c R_C = -\beta \frac{v_{i1}}{2r_{be}} R_c$$

for which the single-ended voltage gain magnitude at either collector is

$$A_{v1} = -\frac{v_o}{v_{i1}} = -\frac{\beta R_c}{2r_{be}} \qquad (2.5.24)$$

5. Common-Mode Operation of Circuit

Whereas a differential amplifier provides large amplification of the difference signal applied to both inputs, it should also provide as small an amplification of the signal common to both inputs. An ac connection showing common input to both transistors is shown in Figure 2.5.16. The ac equivalent circuit is drawn in Figure 2.5.17, from which we can write

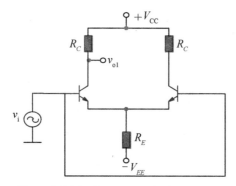

Figure 2.5.16 Common-mode Connection

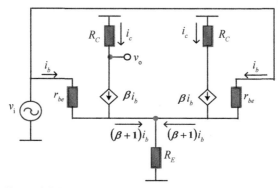

Figure 2.5.17 AC Circuit in Common-mode Connection

2.5 Active Sources and Differential Amplifiers

$$i_b = \frac{v_i - 2(\beta+1)i_b R_E}{r_{be}}$$

which can be rewritten as

$$i_b = \frac{v_i}{r_{be} + 2(\beta+1)R_E}$$

The output voltage magnitude is then

$$v_o = -i_c R_C = -\frac{\beta v_i R_C}{r_{be} + 2(\beta+1)R_E}$$

so a voltage gain is

$$A_c = \frac{v_o}{v_i} = -\frac{\beta R_C}{r_{be} + 2(\beta+1)R_E} \qquad (2.5.25)$$

6. Use of Constant-Current Source

A good differential amplifier has a very large difference gain A_d, which is much larger than the common-mode gain A_c. The common-mode rejection ability of the circuit can be considerably improved by making the common-mode gain as small as possible (ideally, 0). From Equation (10.8), we see that the larger R_E, the smaller A_c. One popular method for increasing the ac value of R_E is using a constant-current source circuit. Figure 2.5.18 shows a differential amplifier with constant-current source to provide a large value of resistance from common emitter to ac ground. The major improvement of this circuit over that in Figure 2.5.9 is the much larger ac impedance for R_E obtained using the constant-current source.

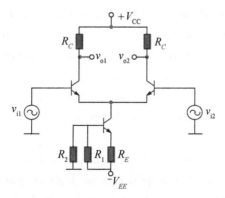

Figure 2.5.18 Differential Amplifier with Constant-current Source

Figure 2.5.19 shows the ac equivalent circuit for the circuit of Figure 2.5.18 when the output is taken from of the collector of Q_1. A practical constant-current source is shown as a high impedance, in parallel with the constant current.

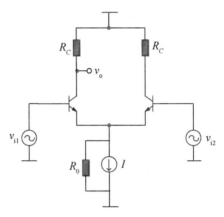

Figure 2.5.19　AC Equivalent of the Circuit of Figure 2.5.18

2.6　Power Amplifiers

The amplifiers discussed in 2.5 operate as input and/or intermediate stages to obtain a large voltage gain or current gain. The transistors within the amplifiers operat in the active region so that their small-signal models are valid. These stages are not required to provide appreciable amounts of power, and the distortion of the output signal is negligible because the transistors operate in the active region.

The requirements for the output stages of audio-frequency power amplifiers are significantly different from those of small-signal low-power amplifiers. An output stage must deliver an appreciable amount of power can be capable of driving low-impedance loads such as loudspeakers. The distortion of the output signal must also be low.

The dc power requirement of an audio amplifier must be as small as possible so that the efficiency of the amplifier is as high as possible. Increasing the efficiency of the amplifier reduces the amount of power dissipated by the transistors and the amount of power drawn from dc supplies, thereby reducing the cost of the power supply and prolonging the life of batteries in battery-powered amplifiers. Also, a low dc power requirement helps to keep the internal junction temperature of the transistors well below the maximum allowable temperature (in the range of 150 ~ 200℃ for silicon devices). As a result, a low dc power requirement minimizes the size of heat sinks and can eliminate the need for cooling fans. Therefore, an output stage should deliver the required amount of power to the load efficiently.

2.6.1 Classification of Power Amplifiers

Power amplifiers are generally classified into four types: class A, class B, class AB, and class C. The classification is based on the shape of the collector current waveform produced by a sinusoidal input signal. In a class A amplifier, the dc biasing collector current I_C of a transistor is higher than the peak amplitude of the ac output current I_p. Thus, the transistor in a class A amplifier conducts during the entire cycle of the input signal, and the conduction angle is $\theta = \omega t = 360°$. That is, the collector current of transistor is given by $i_c = I_C + I_p \sin\omega t$ and $I_C > I_p$. I_p is the peak value of the sinusoidal components of the collector current. The waveform of the collector current for class A operation is shown in Figure 2.6.1(a).

In a class B amplifier, the transistor is biased at zero dc current and conducts for only a half-cycle of the input signal, with a conduction angle of $\theta = \omega t = 180°$. That is, $i_c = I_p \sin\omega t$. The waveform of the collector current for a class B amplifier is shown in Figure 2.6.1(b). The negtative halves of the sinusoid are provided by another transistor that also operates in the class B mode and conducts during the alternate half-cycles.

In a class AB amplifier, the transistor is biased at nonzero dc current that is much smaller than the peak amplitude of the ac output current. The transistor conducts for slightly more than half a cycle of the input signal. The conduction angle is greater than 180° but much less than 360°; that is, $180° < \theta \leqslant 360°$. Thus, $i_c = I_C + I_p \sin\omega t$ and $I_C < I_p$. The waveform of the collector current for a class AB amplifier is shown in Figure 2.6.1(c). The negative halves of the sinusoid are provided by another transistor that also operates in the class AB mode and conducts for an interval slightly greater than the negative half-cycle. The currents from the

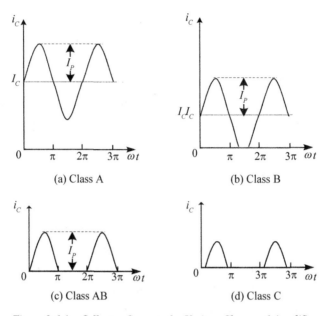

Figure 2.6.1 Collector Currents for Various Classes of Amplifiers

two transistors are combined to form the load current. Both transistors conduct for an interval near the zero crossings of the input signal.

In a class C amplifier, the transitor conducts for an interval shorter than a half-cycle. The conduction angle of the transistor is less than 180°; that is, $\theta <$ 180° and $i_c = I_p \sin\omega t$. The negative halves of the collector current are provided by another transistor. The collector current is of pulsating type and is much more distorted than the current generated by other classes of amplifier. The nonlinear distortion can be filtered out by passing this output through a parallel LC-resonant circuit. The resonant circuit is tuned to the frequency of the input signal an acts as a band-pass filter, giving an output voltage proportional to the amplitude of the fundamental component of the waveform. Class C amplifiers are normally used in radio-frequency applications. Class A and class B amplifiers are commonly used in audio-frequency applications.

Although there are many other types of amplifiers, we will only consider the following kinds: class B push-pull amplifiers, complementary class AB push-pull amplifiers.

2.6.2 Class B Complementary Push-pull Amplifiers

A complementary push-pull amplifier is shown in Figure 2.6.2(a). For $v_I>0$, transistor Q_p remains off and transistor Q_N operates as an emitter follower. For a sufficiently large value of v_I, Q_N saturates and the maximum positive output voltage becomes

$$V_{CE(\max)} = V_{CC} - V_{CE1(\text{sat})} \qquad (2.6.1)$$

For $v_I<0$, transistor Q_N remains off and transistor Q_p operates as an emitter follower. For a sufficiently large negative value of v_I, Q_p saturates and the maximum negative output voltage becomes

$$-V_{CE(\max)} = -(V_{CC} - V_{CE2(\text{sat})}) = -V_{CC} + V_{CE2(\text{sat})} \qquad (2.6.2)$$

Assuming identical transistors of $V_{BE1} = V_{BE2} = V_{BE}$, the output voltage is given by

$$v_o = v_I - V_{BE}, \quad \text{for} \quad -0.7\text{V} \geqslant v_I \geqslant 0.7\text{V} \qquad (2.6.3)$$

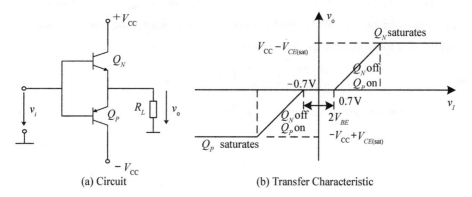

(a) Circuit (b) Transfer Characteristic

Figure 2.6.2 Complementary Class B Push-pull Amplifier

which gives the transfer characteristic of v_o versus v_I as shown in Figure 2.6.2(b). However, during the interval $-0.7\text{V} \geqslant v_I \geqslant 0.7\text{V}$, both Q_N and Q_p remain off, and $v_o = 0$. This cause a dead zone and crossover distortion of the output voltage, as illustrated in Fig 2.6.3.

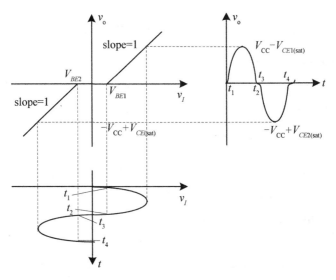

Figure 2.6.3 Crossover Distortion on Input and Output Waveforms

Let us assume that $V_{CE1(\text{sat})} = V_{CE2(\text{sat})} = 0\text{V}$ and $I_{C(\min)} = 0\text{A}$. Assuming a sinusoidal variation in the collector current $i_{c1} = I_p \sin \omega t$, the average collector current of a transistor can be found from

$$I_{c1} = \frac{1}{2\pi}\int_0^\pi i_{c1}\,dt = \frac{1}{2\pi}\int_0^\pi I_p \sin(\omega t)\,d\omega t = \frac{I_p}{\pi}$$

The average current drawn from the dc supply source by transistors Q_N and Q_p is

$$I_{dc} = 2I_{c1} = \frac{2I_p}{\pi}$$

Thus, the average input power supplied from the dc source is

$$P_s = I_{dc}V_{CC} = \frac{2I_p V_{CC}}{\pi} \qquad (2.6.4)$$

The output power is

$$P_L = \frac{I_p^2 R_L}{2} = \frac{I_p V_p}{2} \qquad (2.6.5)$$

Thus, the power efficiency becomes

$$\eta = \frac{P_L}{P_s} = \frac{\frac{I_p V_p}{2}}{\frac{2 I_p V_{CC}}{\pi}} = \frac{\pi}{4}\left(\frac{V_p}{V_{CC}}\right) \quad (2.6.6)$$

which gives $\eta = 50\%$ at $V_p = 2V_{CC}/\pi$ and $\eta = 78.5\%$ at $V_p = V_{CC}$, the maximum output power is given by

$$P_{L(\max)} = \frac{I_p^2 R_L}{2} = \frac{I_p V_p}{2} = \frac{I_p V_{CC}}{2} = \frac{V_{CC}^2}{2R_L} \quad (2.6.7)$$

Thus, the maximum power efficiency is

$$\eta = \frac{P_{L(\max)}}{P_s} = \frac{I_p V_{CC}/2}{2 I_p V_{CC}/\pi} = \frac{\pi}{4} = 78.5\% \quad (2.6.8)$$

Therefore, the maximum efficiency of a complementary push-pull class B amplifier is much higher than that of a class A amplifier.

2.6.3 Complementary Class AB Push-Pull Amplifiers

The crossover distortion of a complementary class B push-pull amplifier is minimized or eliminated in a class AB amplifier, in which the transistors operate in the active region when the input voltage v_I is small ($v_I \approx 0$). The transistors are biased in such a way that each transistor conducts for a small quiescent current I_Q at $v_I = 0$V. A biasing circuit is shown in Figure 2.6.4 (a). A biasing voltage V_{BB} is applied between the bases of Q_N and Q_p. For $v_I = 0$V, a voltage $V_{BB}/2$ appears across the base-emitter junction of each Q_N and Q_p. Choosing $V_{BB}/2 = V_{BEN} = V_{EBP}$

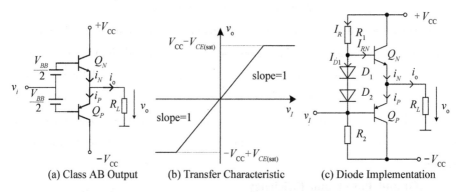

Figure 2.6.4 Elimination of the Dead Zone in a Class AB Amplifier

will ensure that both transistors will be on the verge of conducting. That is, $v_O = 0$ for $v_I = 0$V. A small positive input voltage v_I will then cause Q_N to conduct; similarly, a small negative input voltage will cause Q_p to conduct.

1. Transfer Characteristic

The output voltage v_O is given by

$$v_O = v_I + \frac{V_{BB}}{2} - V_{BEN}(=V_{EBP}) \tag{2.6.9}$$

which, for identical transistors of $V_{BEN} = V_{EBP}$ and $\frac{V_{BB}}{2} = V_{BEN}$, gives $v_O = v_I$.

Therefore, most of the crossover distortion is eliminated. The transfer characteristic is shown in Figure 2.6.4(b). For positive v_O, a current i_O flows through R_L. That is,

$$i_N = i_P + i_O$$

Any increase in i_N will cause a corresponding increase in V_{BEN} above the quiescent value of $V_{BB}/2$. Since V_{BB} must remain constant, the increasing in V_{BEN} will cause an equal decrease in V_{EBP} and hence in i_p. Thus,

$$V_{BB} = V_{BEN} + V_{EBP}$$

which, expressed in terms of saturation current I_S, becomes

$$2V_T \ln \frac{I_Q}{I_S} = V_T \ln \frac{i_N}{I_S} + V_T \ln \frac{i_P}{i_S}$$

After simplification, we get

$$I_Q^2 = i_N i_P = i_N(i_N - i_O) = i_N^2 - i_N i_O$$

which can be solved for the current i_N for a given quiescent current I_Q. Thus, as i_N increases, i_P decreases by the same ratio. However, their product remains constant. As v_I becomes positive, Q_N acts as an emitter follower delivering output power, and Q_p is cut off. When v_I becomes negative, the opposite occurs: Q_p acts as an emitter follower, and v_O follows the input signal v_I. The circuit operates in class AB mode, because both transistors remain on and operate in the active region.

2. Output Power and Efficiency

The power relationships in class AB amplifiers are identical to those in class B amplifiers, except that the class AB circuit dissipates a quiescent power of $I_Q V_{CC}$ for every transistor. Thus, from Equation 2.6.4, we can find the average power supplied from the dc source as

$$P_S = \frac{2I_P V_{CC}}{\pi} + I_Q V_{CC} = V_{CC}\left(I_Q + \frac{2I_P}{\pi}\right) \qquad (2.6.10)$$

3. Biasing with Diodes

The biasing circuit in Figure 2.6.4 (a) has a serious problem when the temperatures of Q_N and Q_P increase as a result of their power dissipation. Recall that the value of V_{BE} for a given current falls with temperature at approximately 2.5mV/℃. Thus, if the biasing voltage $V_{BB}/2$ remains constant with temperature, $V_{BE} = V_{BB}/2$ also holds constant and the collector current will increase as temperature increases. The increase in the collector current increases the power dissipation, in turn increasing the collector current and causing the temperature to rise further. This phenomenon, in which a positive feedback mechanism leads to excessive temperature rise, is called thermal runaway. Thermal runaway can ultimately lead to the destruction of the transistors unless they are protected.

In order to avoid thermal runaway, the biasing voltages must decrease as the temperature increases. One solution is to use diodes that have a compensating effect, as shown in Figure 2.6.4(c). The diodes must be in close contact with the output transistors so that their temperature will increase by the same amount as that of Q_N and Q_P. Therefore, in a discrete circuit, the diodes should be mounted on the metal of Q_N or Q_P. Since resistances R_1 and R_2 provide the quiescent current I_Q for the transistors and also ensure that the diodes conduct, to guarantee the base biasing current for Q_N when the load current becomes maximum.

Summary

Bipolar junction transistors (BJTs) are active devices, and they are of two types: npn and, pnp. BJTs are current-controlled devices; the output depends on the input current. A BJT can operate in any one of three regions: the cutoff, active, or saturation region. The forward current β, which is a very important parameter, and the ratio of the collector current to the base current. The biasing circuit sets the operating point such that the influences of parameter variations are minimized and allows for the superposition of AC signals with minimum distortion. BJTs may be represented by linear or nonlinear models. The linear models, which give approximate results, are commonly used for initial design and analysis.

A common-emitter amplifier is used for voltage amplification. Emitter resistance input resistance, but it reduces voltage gain. A compromise is normally made between high input resistance and high voltage gain requirements. A common-collector amplifier, which is known as an emitter follower, offers a high input resistance and a low output resistance, with a gain approaching unity.

FETs, which are voltage-controlled devices, have many advantages over BJTs. FETs are of two types: junction FETs and MOSFETs. MOSFETs also are of two types: enhancement and depletion. Each type can be either P-channel or n-channel. Depending on the value of the drain-source voltage, an FET can operate in one of three regions: ohmic, saturation, or cutoff. In the ohmic region, an FET is operated as a voltage-controlled device. In the saturation region, an FET is operated as an amplifier. An enhancement MOSFET conducts only when the gate-source voltage exceeds the threshold voltage. Because of a reverse-biased pn-junction, a small gate current (on the order of μA) flows through JFETs. The gate current of a MOSFET is very small (on the order of nA). FETs should be biased properly to set the gate-source voltage in appropriate polarity and magnitude. The Q-point should be stable, and a biasing circuit should be designed to minimize the influences of parameter variations. MOSFETs are widely used in very-large-scale integrated (VLSI) circuits.

Problems

2.1 What is the major difference between a bipolar and a unipolar device?

2.2 If the emitter current of a transistor is 8mA and I_B is 1/100 of I_C, determine the levels of I_C and I_B.

2.3 From memory, sketch the transistor symbol for a pnp and an npn transistor, and then insert the conventional flow direction for each current.

2.4 Measured by two electrodes in the current amplification circuit of two transistors is shown in Figure p2.4 Question: (1) Calculate the other electrode current and mark the actual directions in the diagram. (2) Determine whether the transistor is an NPN or a PNP transistor, mark e, c, b.

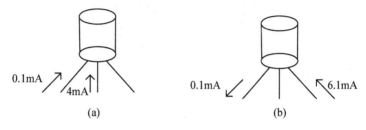

Figure p2.4

2.5 Measured in a amplifier circuit of three electrodes A, B, C, respectively, to ground potential $V_A=-9V$, $V_B=-6V$, $V_C=-6.2V$, analyze A, B, C which is the base, emitter, collector, and describe whether the transistor is an NPN or a PNP transistor.

2.6 Measured in a amplifier circuit of three electrodes potential is shown in the Figure p2.6, determine what state do these transistors work in.

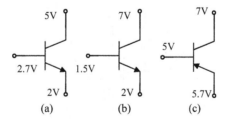

Figure p2.6

2.7 Determine the following for the fixed-bias configuration of Figure 2.7:
    a. I_{BQ} and I_{CQ}.
    b. V_{CEQ}.

c. V_B and V_C.
d. V_{BC}.

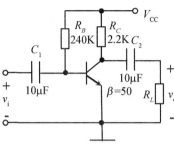

Figure p2.7

2.8 For the emitter bias network of Figure p2.8, determine:
a. I_B
b. I_C
c. V_{CE}
d. V_C
e. V_E
f. V_B
g. V_{BC}

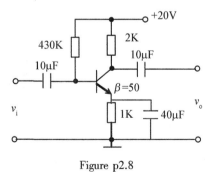

Figure p2.8

2.9 The parameters of the amplifier circuit in Figure p2.9 are $V_{CC} = 5V$,

$R_C = 500\Omega$, $R_1 = 6.5\text{k}\Omega$, $R_2 = 2.5\text{k}\Omega$, $R_E = 450\Omega$, $R_S = 500\Omega$, $R_L = 5\text{k}\Omega$. Assume $\beta = 100$.

(a) Find the Q-point defined by I_B, I_C, and V_{CE}.
(b) Calculate A_V, R_i, R_o.

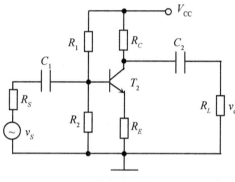

Figure p2.9

2.10 For the network of Figure p2.10, determine:

a. r_e.
b. Z_i.
c. Z_o.
d. A_v.

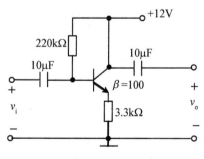

Figure p2.10

2.11 The amplifier circuits in Figure p2.11, find A_V, R_i, R_o.

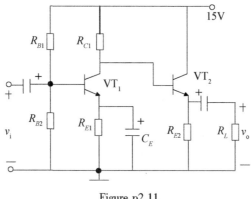

Figure p2.11

2.12 Calculate the dc voltages and currents in the circuit of Figure p2.12.

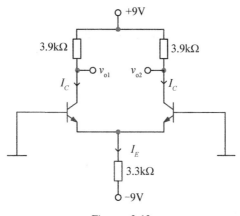

Figure p2.12

2.13 As is shown in the Figure p2.13, circuit C capacity is large enough.
(1) What kind of amplifier circuit do this circuit belong to?
(2) Supposing that $R_L = 8\Omega$, V_{CES} can be ignored, if requested maximum undistorted output power (ignoring crossover distortion) of 9W, the supply voltage

is at least as much?

(3) Supposing that $V_{CC} = 22\text{V}$, $R_L = 8\Omega$, $|V_{CES}| = 2\text{V}$, estimate the maximum output power of the circuit.

2.14 The circuit is shown in Figure p2.14:

(1) When the input signal $V_i = 10\text{V}$ (RMS), calculate the circuit output power P_o and efficiency η.

(2) When the amplitude of the input signal $V_{im} = V_{CC} = 20\text{V}$, calculate P_o and η.

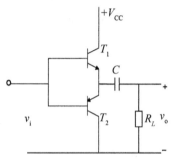

Figure p2.13

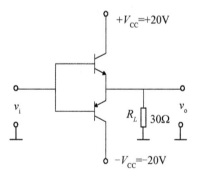

Figure p2.14

2.15 Figure p2.15 shows the saturation voltage drop of tube T_1 and T_2 $|V_{CES}| = 3\text{V}$, $V_{CC} = 15\text{V}$, $R_L = 8\Omega$. (1) What do D_1 and D_2 in the circuit function as? (2) In static state, determine the emitter potential V_{EQ}. (3) Determine P_{OM} and η?

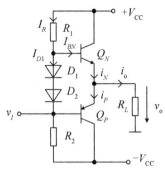

Figure p2.15

Chapter 3

Feedback Amplifiers

3.1 The Basic Concept of Feedback Amplifiers

Feedback is commonly used in amplifier circuits. A signal that is proportional to the output is compared with an input or a reference signal so that a desired output is obtained from the amplifier. The difference between the input and the feedback signals, called the error signal, is amplified by the amplifier. There are two types of feedbacks:

In negative feedback, the output signal (or a fraction of it) is continuously fed back to the input side and is subtracted from the input signal to create an error signal, which is then corrected by the amplifier to produce the desired output signal.

In positive feedback, the output signal (or a fraction of it) is continuously fed back to the input and added to the input signal to create a larger error signal, which is then amplified to produce a larger output until the output reaches the saturation voltage limit of the amplifier.

In negative feedback, the signal that is fed back to the input side is known as the feedback signal, and its polarity is opposite that of the input signal, that is, it is out of phase by 180° with respect to the input signal. Negative feedback in an amplifier has four major benefits: (1) It stabilizes the overall gain of an amplifier with respect to parameter variations due to temperature, supply voltage, etc.; (2) it increases or decreases the input and output impedances; (3) it reduces the distortion and the effect of nonlinearity; and (4) it increases the bandwidth. There are two disadvantages of negative feedback: (1) The overall gain is reduced almost in direct proportion to the benefits, and it is often necessary compensate for the decrease in gain by adding an extra amplifier stage; and (2) A careful design is required to overcome the tend to oscillate.

3.2 The Principle of Negative Feedback

Figure 3.2.1 shows the block diagram of a generalized feedback circuit. This diagram can be used to represent any feedback situation, positive or negative feedback, amplifiers or other types of systems. In this general system, x is electronic variable, which may be a current or voltage. The output signal x_o is passed through a feedback network F to create a feedback signal x_f. Signal x_o is caused by applying the input signal x_i through a summing circuit to give x_d at the input of the forward amplifier unit A.

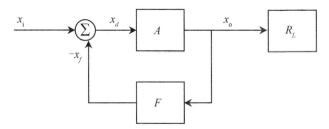

Figure 3.2.1 Amplifier with Negative Feedback Applied

The feedback signal x_f is added to the input signal x_i in the summing circuit. If x_f is in phase with x_i, it will add to x_i, making x_d larger than x_i and resulting in positive feedback and possible oscillations. If x_f is out of phase with (of the opposite polarity to) x_i, it will subtract from x_i to make x_d smaller than x_i, and negative feedback will result.

Note that the phase inversion for negative feedback may occur in A, or F in the summing circuit.

The amplifier A and the feedback network F are connected so that they form a signal loop within the circuit. The gain of the forward amplifier unit is defined as

$$A = \frac{x_o}{x_d} \qquad (3.2.1)$$

and may be a voltage gain, a current gain, a transconductance, or a transresistance. When feedback is applied, the gain of the amplifier is defined as

$$A_f = \frac{x_o}{x_i} \qquad (3.2.2)$$

where x_o is the load variable being delivered by the forward amplifier and is the variable being sampled by the feedback network.

The feedback factor may now be defined as

$$F = \frac{x_f}{x_o} \qquad (3.2.3)$$

The variables applied to the summing point (x_i, x_f, and x_d) all have the same units, so that for negative feedback

$$x_d = x_i - x_f \qquad (3.2.4)$$

Combining Equations (3.2.1), (3.2.3), and (3.2.4) to eliminate x_d and x_f yields

$$x_o = A(x_i - Fx_o) \qquad (3.2.5)$$

Now solving this for the ratio x_o/x_i and substituting into Equation (3.2.2) gives

$$A_f = \frac{x_o}{x_i} = \frac{A}{1+AF} = \frac{A}{T} \qquad (3.2.6)$$

where the loop gain is defined as

$$T = AF \qquad (3.2.7)$$

If the loop gain $|AF|$ is made much greater than unity, then Equation (3.2.6) becomes approximately

$$A_f = \frac{1}{F} \quad (\text{for } |AF| \gg 1) \qquad (3.2.8)$$

Under these conditions the feedback signal x_f is almost as large as the input signal x_i so that the difference signal x_d becomes a very small quantity. The overall gain is almost a reciprocal of F, which can be comprised of very stable passive components, and is almost completely independent of changes in the amplifier gain A.

3.3 Feedback Topologies

The feedback of Figure 3.2.1 represents a general form; it does not indicate whether the input and output signals are voltages or currents. In practical amplifiers, the input and output signals can be either voltages or currents. If the output voltage is the feedback signal, it can be either compared with the input voltage to generate the error voltage signal or compared with the input current to generate the error current signal. Similarly, the output current can be fed back and either compared with the input voltage to generate the error voltage signal or compared with the input current to generate the error current signal. Therefore, there are four feedback configurations, depending on whether the input and output signals are voltages or currents. These configurations are series-voltage feedback, series-current feedback, parallel-voltage feedback and parallel-current feedback shown in Figure 3.3.1.

In series-voltage feedback, as shown in Figure 3.3.1(a), the output variable $x_o = v_o$ is the input to the feedback network, and the feedback variable $x_f = v_f$ is proportional to the output voltage v_o. The feedback network forms a series circuit with the input voltage v_i but a parallel circuit with the output voltage v_o. That is, $v_i - v_f = v_e$.

$$A = \frac{x_o}{x_d} = \frac{v_o}{v_d} = A_v \quad \text{(is voltage gain)}$$

$$F = \frac{x_f}{x_o} = \frac{v_f}{v_o} = F_v \tag{3.3.1}$$

In series-current feedback, as shown in Figure 3.3.1(b), the output variable $x_o = i_o$ is the input to the feedback network, and the feedback variable $x_f = v_f$ is proportional to the output current i_o. The feedback network forms a series circuit with the input voltage v_i and the output current i_o. That is, $v_i - v_f = v_e$.

$$A = \frac{x_o}{x_d} = \frac{i_o}{v_d} = A_g \quad \text{(is transconductance)}$$

$$F = \frac{x_f}{x_o} = \frac{v_f}{i_o} = F_r \tag{3.3.2}$$

In parallel-voltage feedback, as shown in Figure 3.3.1(c), the output variable $x_o = v_o$ is also the input to the feedback network, and the feedback variable $x_f = i_f$ is proportional to the output voltage v_o. The feedback network is in parallel circuit with the both input and output voltages. The input current i_i is shared by the amplifier and the feedback network. That is, $i_i - i_f = i_d$.

3.3 Feedback Topologies

$$A = \frac{x_o}{x_d} = \frac{v_o}{i_d} = A_r \quad (\text{is ransresistance})$$

$$F = \frac{x_f}{x_o} = \frac{i_f}{v_o} = F_g$$

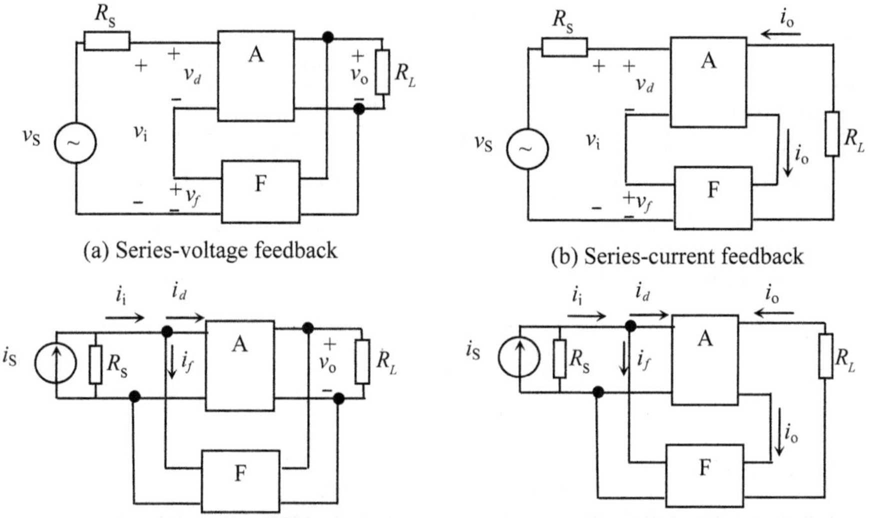

(a) Series-voltage feedback

(b) Series-current feedback

(c) Parallel-voltage feedback

(d) Parallel-current feedback

Figure 3.3.1 Feedback Configurations

In parallel-current feedback, as shown in Figure 3.3.1(d), the output variable $x_o = i_o$ is the input to the feedback network, and the feedback variable $x_f = i_f$ is proportional to the output current i_o. The feedback network is in parallel circuit with the input voltage but in series with output current. The input current i_i is shared by the amplifier and the feedback network. That is, $i_i - i_f = i_d$.

$$A = \frac{x_o}{x_d} = \frac{i_o}{i_d} = A_i \quad (\text{is current gain})$$

$$F = \frac{x_f}{x_o} = \frac{i_f}{i_o} = F_i$$

There are two circuits in a feedback amplifier: the amplifier circuits (or A circuit) and the feedback (or F circuit). The effective gain is always decreased by a factor of $(1 + AF)$. In series-type arrangements, both A and F circuits are connected in series, and the effective resistance is increased by a factor of $(1+AF)$. In parallel-type arrangements, both A and F circuits are connected in parallel, and the effective resistance is decreased by a factor of $(1+AF)$. The effects of different types of feedback are summarized in Table 3.1.1.

Table 3.1.1

	Gain	Input resistance	Output resistance
Without feedback	A	R_i	R_o
Series-voltage	$A_{vf}=\dfrac{A_V}{1+A_V F_V}$	$R_{if}=R_i(1+A_v F_v)$	$R_{of}=\dfrac{R_o}{1+A_V F_V}$
Series-current	$A_{gf}=\dfrac{A_g}{1+A_g F_r}$	$R_{if}=R_i(1+A_g F_r)$	$R_{of}=R_o(1+A_g F_r)$
Parallel-voltage	$A_{rf}=\dfrac{A_r}{1+A_r F_g}$	$R_{if}=\dfrac{R_i}{1+A_r F_g}$	$R_{of}=\dfrac{R_o}{1+A_r F_g}$
Parallel-current	$A_{if}=\dfrac{A_i}{1+A_i F_i}$	$R_{if}=\dfrac{R_i}{1+A_i F_i}$	$R_{of}=R_o(1+A_i F_i)$

3.4 Identifying the Type of Negative Feedback Amplifier

Depending on the type of feedback, amplifier has different characteristics. So we must judge the type of negative feedback amplifier firstly. The analysis can be simplified by following steps:

Step 1: Identify the feedback network.

Generally, feedback network is across input and output loop, for example, R_B in Figure 3.4.1 (a), R_E in Figure 3.4.1 (b) and R_f in Figure 3.4.1 (c).

Step 2: Identify the polarity of feedback network.

Firstly, the polarity of input signal is assumed in positive, according to the polarity relationship of three electrodes in triode shown in Figure 3.4.2, we can judge the out put polarity of triode. Note that the polarity relationship of three electrodes in pnp triode is the same as that in npn triode.

3.4 Identifying the Type of Negative Feedback Amplifier

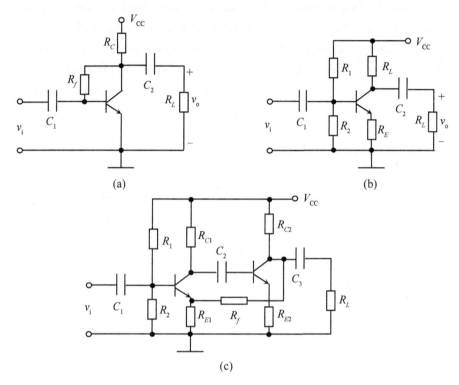

Figure 3.4.1 Feedback Circuits

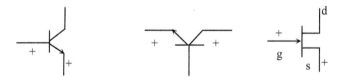

Figure 3.4.2 The Polarity Relationship of Three Electrodes

Secondly, identify the polarity of feedback signal. If the polarity of feedback signal decrease input signal, the polarity of feedback network is negative. Otherwise, it is positive.

Step 3: Identify the type of feedback network.

a. Get the input terminal short-circuited, if feedback network disappears, the network is a parallel feedback; otherwise, it is a series feedback.

b. Get the Output terminal short-circuited, if feedback network disappears, the network is a voltage feedback; otherwise, it is a current feedback.

Using the above judging method, we know Figure 3.4.1 (a) is a parallel-voltage negative feedback amplifier, Figure 3.4.1 (b) is a series-current negative feedback amplifier and Figure 3.4.1 (c) is a series-voltage negative feedback amplifier.

3.5 Approximate Calculation of A_f

From Equation (3.6), we have known under the condition of $|AF| \gg 1$, $A_f \approx \dfrac{1}{F}$. So when we want to obtain A_f, feedback factor F must be found firstly.

Steps to find F:

a. Identify the type of feedback network.

b. If the feedback is series type, the link of triode and feedback network should be oper-circuited to find v_f, so $F = \dfrac{v_f}{x_o}$. If the feedback is parallel type, the input terminal should be short-circuited to find i_f, so $F = \dfrac{i_f}{x_o}$.

For example, the circuit is shown in Figure 3.4.1 (c). It is series-voltage negative feedback. So the link of triode and feedback network should be oper-circuited,

$$v_f = v_{E1} = \frac{R_{E1}}{R_{E1}+R_f} v_o$$

$$F_v = \frac{x_f}{x_o} = \frac{v_f}{v_o} = \frac{R_{E1}}{R_{E1}+R_f}$$

So

$$A_{vf} = \frac{1}{F_v} = 1 + \frac{R_f}{R_{E1}}$$

Summary

There are two types of feedback: negative feedback and positive feedback. Negative feedback is normally used in amplifier circuits, and positive feedback is applied exclusively in oscillators. Negative feedback has certain advantages, such as stabilization of overall gain with respect to parameter variations, reduction of distortion, reduction of the effects of nonlinearity, and increase in bandwidth.

However, these advantages are obtained at the expense of gain reduction, and additional amplifier stages may be required to make up the gain reduction. If the loop gain $AF \gg 1$, the overall (or closed-loop) gain depends inversely on the feedback factor F and is directly sensitive to changes in the feedback factor.

Problems

3.1 Identifying the type of negative feedback amplifiers shown in Figure p3.1.

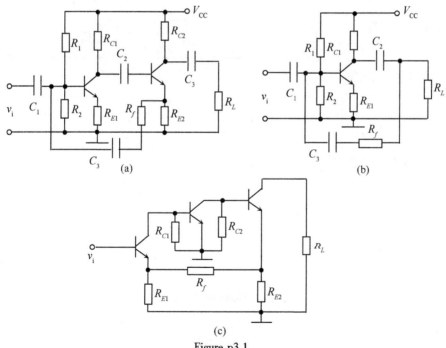

Figure p3.1

3.2 Identifying the type of negative feedback amplifiers shown in Figure p3.2.

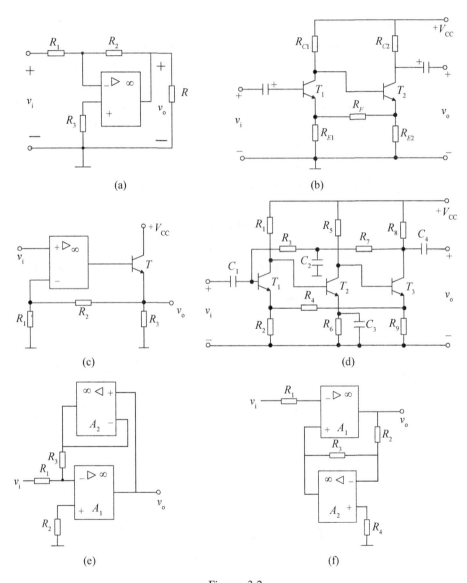

Figure p3.2

3.3 If an amplifier with gain of -1000 and feedback of $F = -0.1$ has a gain change of 20% due to temperature, calculate the change in gain of the feedback amplifier.

3.4 Calculate the gain of a negative-feedback amplifier having $A = -2000$ and $F = -\dfrac{1}{10}$.

Chapter 4

Oscillators

An amplifier with negative feedback will be unstable if the magnitude of the loop gain is greater than or equal to 1 and its phase shift is $\pm 180°$. Under these conditions, the feedback becomes positive and the output of the amplifier oscillates. An oscillator is a circuit that generates a repetitive waveform of fixed amplitude at a fixed frequency without any external input signal. A waveform of this characteristic can be obtained by applying positive feedback in amplifiers. Positive feedback provides enough feedback signal to maintain oscillations. Although oscillations are very undesirable in linear amplifier circuits, oscillators are designed specifically to produce controlled and predictable oscillation. Thus, the strategy for designing oscillators is quite different from that for designing linear amplifiers. Occasionally, oscillators have inputs that are used to control the frequency or to synchronize the oscillations with an external reference. Oscillators are used in many electronic circuits, such as radios, televisions, computers, and communication equipment.

4.1 Principles of Oscillators

An oscillator is an amplifier with positive feedback. The block diagram of an amplifier with positive feedback, as show in Figure 4.1.1(a), suggests the following relationships:

$$x_d = x_i + x_f$$
$$x_o = A x_d$$
$$x_f = F x_o$$

Using these relationships, we get the closed-loop voltage gain A_f

$$A_f = \frac{x_o}{x_i} = \frac{A}{1-AF} \quad (4.1.1)$$

which can be made very large by setting $1-AF=0$. That is, an output of reasonable magnitude can be obtained with a very small-value input signal, tending to zero, as shown in Figure 4.1.1(b). Thus, the amplifier will be unstable when $1-AF=0$, which gives the loop gain as

$$AF = 1 \qquad (4.1.2)$$

Expressing Equation (4.1.2) in polar form, yields

$$AF = 1 \angle 0° \text{ or } 1 \angle 360°$$

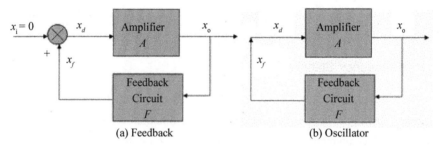

Figure 4.1.1   Oscillator Block Diagram

The above discussion leads to the following design criteria for oscillators:

(1) The magnitude of the loop gain must be unity or slightly larger at the desired oscillation frequency.

(2) The total phase shift of the loop gain must be equal to 0° or 360° at the same frequency.

(3) The first two conditions must not be satisfied at other frequencies. This condition is normally met by carefully selecting the component values.

(4) The first two conditions must continue to be satisfied as parameter values change in response to component tolerance, temperature change, aging and device replacement. Meeting this criterion often requires special design considerations.

If an amplifier provides a phase shift of 180°, the feedback circuit must provide an additional phase shift of 180° so that the total phase shift around the loop is 360°. The type of waveform generated by an oscillator depends on the types of components used in the circuit; hence the waveform may be sinusoidal, square, or triangular. The frequency of oscillation is determined by the feedback components.

RC components generate a sinusoidal waveform at audio frequencies—that is, in the range from several hertz(Hz) to several kilohertz(kHz).

LC components generate a square wave at radio frequencies, i.e. from 100kHz to 100MHz.

Crystals generate a triangular or sawtooth wave over a wide range, i.e. from 10kHz, to 10MHz.

Oscillators can be classified into many types depending on the feedback components, amplifiers, and circuit topologies used. This chapter will cover the following types of oscillators: phase-shift oscillators, Wien-bridge oscillators, Colpitts oscillators, Hartley oscillators, and crystal oscillators.

4.1.1 Frequency Stability

The ability of an oscillator to oscillate at an exact frequency is called frequency stability. The oscillating frequency is a function of circuit components for example, LC components and can change in response to temperature changes, device replacement, or parasitic elements. Good frequency stability can be obtained by making the phase shift a strong function of frequency at resonance. That is, $|d\Phi/d\omega|$ (at $\omega=\omega_0$) is made large so that only a slight change in ω is required to correct any phase shift and restore the loop gain to zero phase shift.

The qualify factor Q of a circuit also determines the frequency stability. The higher Q, the better the stability, because the variation in phase shift with frequency near resonance is greater. Crystal oscillators are far more stable than RC or LC oscillators, especially at higher frequencies. The equivalent electrical circuit of a crystal has a very high Q value, leading to a high value of $d\Phi/d\omega$. LC and crystal oscillators are generally used for the generation of high-frequency signals; RC oscillators are used mostly for audio-frequency applications.

4.1.2 Amplitude Stability

Like the frequency, the gain of practical amplifiers can change in response to changes in parameters such as temperature, age, and operating point. Therefore, $|AF|$ might drop below unity. If the magnitude of AF falls below unity, an oscillating circuit ceases oscillating. In practice, an osciator is designed with a value of $|AF|$ that is slightly higher than unity—say, by 5%–at the oscillating frequency. The greater the value of $|AF|$, the greater the amplitude of the output signal and the amount of its distortion. This distortion will usually lower the gain A to the value required to sustain oscillation.

For good stability, the change in the gain A with a change in the amplitude of output voltage should be made large; an increase in amplitude must result in a decrease in gain. That is, dA/dx_o must be a large negative number. An oscillator is often stabilized by adding nonlinear limiting devices or elements such as diodes.

4.2 Phase-Shift Oscillators

A phase-shift oscillator consists of an inverting amplifier with a positive feedback circuit. The amplifier gives a phase shift of 180° and the feedback circuit gives another phase shift of 180°, so that the total phase shift around the loop is 360°. A phase-shift oscillator consisting of an inverting op-amp amplifier with positive feedback is shown in Figure 4.2.1 The feedback circuit provides voltage feedback from the output back to the input of the amplifier. Any signal that appears at the inverting terminal is shifted by 180°, shift is required for oscillation at a specific frequency in order to give a total phase shift around the loop of 360°. Since the feedback network consists of the resistors and the capacitors, as show in Figure 4.2.1(b), this type of oscillator is also known as an RC oscillator. The transfer

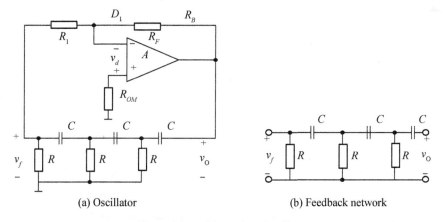

Figure 4.2.1 Phase-shift Oscillator

function of the feedback network is given by

$$F(s) = \frac{V_f(s)}{V_o(s)} = \frac{R^3 C^3 s^3}{R^3 C^3 s^3 + 6R^2 C^2 s^2 + 5RCs + 1} \quad (4.2.1)$$

The closed-loop voltage gain of the op-amp circuit is

$$A(s) = \frac{V_o(s)}{V_f(s)} = -\frac{R_F}{R_1} \quad (4.2.2)$$

Since $AF = 1$ for an oscillator, from Equations (4.2.1) and (4.2.2), we get

$$-\frac{R_F}{R_1} \left(\frac{R^3 C^3 s^3}{R^3 C^3 s^3 + 6R^2 C^2 s^2 + 5RCs + 1} \right) = 1 \quad (4.2.3)$$

Substituting $s = j\omega$ into Equation (4.2.3) and canceling the elements in the denominator, gives

$$-R_F(-jR^3 C^3 \omega^3) = R_1(-jR^3 C^3 \omega^3 - 6R^2 C^2 \omega^2 + j5RC\omega + 1)$$

Letting the real part on the right side in the above equation yields

$$R_1(-6R^2 C^2 \omega^2 + 1) = 0$$

which gives the oscillation frequency ω_0 as

$$\omega_0 = \omega = 2\pi f_0 = \frac{1}{\sqrt{6} RC} \quad \text{(in rad/s)} \quad (4.2.4)$$

where f_0 is the frequency in Hz. Equating the imaginary parts on both sides yields

$$-R_F(-jR^3 C^3 \omega^3) = R_1(-jR^3 C^3 \omega^3 + j5RC\omega)$$

which gives

$$R_F = R_1 \left(\frac{5}{R^2 C^2 \omega^2} - 1 \right) \quad (4.2.5)$$

Substituting the value of $\omega = \omega_0$ from Equation (4.2.4) into Equation (4.2.5) yields

$$\frac{R_F}{R_1} = 29 \quad (4.2.6)$$

which gives the condition for sustained oscillations. This relationship does not control the peak amplitude of the output voltage. The oscillation frequency in Equation (4.2.4) is inversely proportional to the RC product, assuming that both resistances and capacitances are equal. Theoretically, the frequency can be varied by varying either R or C. In practice, it is usually easier to vary R on a continuous basis and to vary C on a discrete basis. Identical capacitors are switched into the circuit at each frequency range. Also, identical resistances, which together are referred to as a gauged potentiometer, are mounted on the same shaft and are used to vary the frequency on a continuous basis in each frequency range.

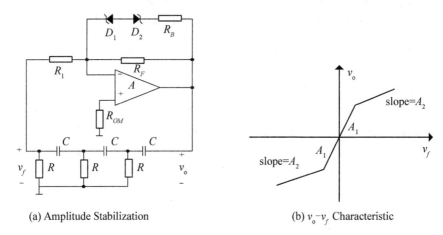

(a) Amplitude Stabilization

(b) v_o-v_f Characteristic

Figure 4.2.2 Stabilization of a Phase-shift Oscillator

Note that setting the loop gain to unity is not a reliable method for designing an oscillator. To stabilize an oscillator, usually it is necessary to limit the output voltage by introducing nonlinearity. Stability can be achieved by adding two zener diodes in series with a resistance, as shown in Figure 4.2.2. As long as the magnitude of the voltage v_f across R_1 is less than the zener breakdown voltage, the zener diodes act as an open circuit, and the gain of the amplifier is

$$|A_1| = \frac{R_F}{R_1} \quad (4.2.7)$$

As soon as the magnitude of v_f starts to increase above V_Z, the zener diodes conduct, and the resistor R_B suddenly becomes in parallel with R_F so that the gain is reduced. The new gain becomes

$$|A_2| = \frac{R_F // R_B}{R_1} \quad (4.2.8)$$

which is less than $|A_1|$. Furthermore, if the output amplitude starts to decrease, the gain $|A|$ is increased again. The v_o-v_f characteristic of the amplifier is shown in Figure 4.4.2(b).

EXAMPLE 1 Design the phase-shift oscillator shown in Figure 4.2.1 so that the oscillating frequency is $f_0 = 400$Hz.

SOLUTION The following steps can be used to complete the design:

Step 1: Choose a suitable value of C: Let $C = 0.1\mu F$

Step 2: Calculate the value of R from Equation (4.2.4):

$$R = \frac{1}{2\pi\sqrt{6}f_0 C} = \frac{1}{2\pi \times \sqrt{6} \times 400 \times 0.1\mu F} = 1624\Omega.$$

Choose $R = 1.7k\Omega$ (use a 2.7kΩ potentiometer)

Step 3: To prevent the loading of the op-amp by the RC network, choose R_1 much larger than R by making $R_1 \geq 10R$. Therefore, let

$$R_1 = 10R = 10 \times 1.7k\Omega = 17k\Omega$$

Step 4: Choose the value of R_F from Equation (4.2.6).

Choose a 500kΩ potentiometer R_F to account for tolerance.

4.3 Wien-Bridge Oscillators

A Wien bridge, as shown in Figure 4.3.1 is used for making measurements of unknown resistors or capacitors. The bridge has a series RC network in one arm and a parallel RC network in the adjoining arm. R_1 and R_F are connected in two other arms. While the bridge is making measurements, either R_1 or R_F acts as a calibrated resistor; the resistance is varied until the null voltage $v_d = 0$ is found. If all component values are known except one, the value of that one can be determined from the following relation:

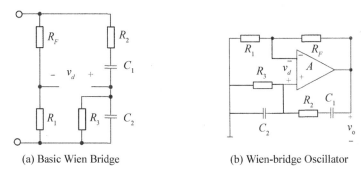

(a) Basic Wien Bridge (b) Wien-bridge Oscillator

Figure 4.3.1 Wien Bridge

$$\frac{R_2}{R_3}+\frac{C_2}{C_1}=\frac{R_F}{R_1} \qquad (4.3.1)$$

If an op-amp is inserted into the basic bridge, as shown in Figure 4.3.1(b), the bridge is known as a Wien-bridge oscillator, provided the elements are adjusted so that $R_2 = R_3 = R$ and $C_1 = C_2 = C$. The op-amp, along with R_1 and R_F, operates as a noninverting amplifier, as shown in Figure 4.3.2(a). The Wien-bridge oscillator is one of the most commonly used audio-frequency oscillators.

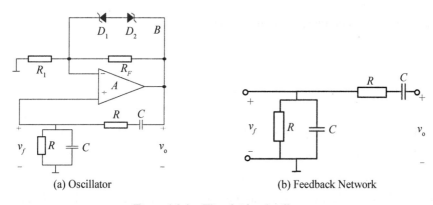

Figure 4.3.2 Wien-bridge Oscillator

The transfer function of the feedback network shown in Figure 4.3.2(b) is given by

$$F(s)=\frac{V_f(s)}{V_o(s)}=\frac{RCs}{R^2C^2s^2+3RCs+1} \qquad (4.3.2)$$

The closed-loop voltage gain of the noninverting amplifier is given by

$$A(s)=\frac{V_o(s)}{V_f(s)}=1+\frac{R_F}{R_1} \qquad (4.3.3)$$

For an oscillator, $AF=1$. Using Equations (4.3.2) and (4.3.3), we get

$$\left(1+\frac{R_F}{R_1}\right)\frac{RCs}{R^2C^2s^2+3RCs+1}=1 \qquad (4.3.4)$$

Substituting $s=j\omega$ into Equation (4.3.4), we get

$$\left(1+\frac{R_F}{R_1}\right)jRC\omega=-R^2C^2\omega^2+j3RC\omega+1$$

Letting real parts on the left side equal those on the right side, gives
$$0 = -R^2 C^2 \omega^2 + 1$$
which gives the oscillation frequency as

$$f_0 = \frac{1}{2\pi RC} \quad (\text{in Hz}) \qquad (4.3.5)$$

Letting imaginary parts on the left side equal those on the right side, yields
$$\left(1 + \frac{R_F}{R_1}\right) jRC\omega = j3RC\omega$$
which gives the condition for oscillation as
$$1 + \frac{R_F}{R_1} = 3$$

or
$$\frac{R_F}{R_1} = 2 \qquad (4.3.6)$$

For stabilization, a power-sensitive resistor such as a lamp or a thermistor is usually used to dynamically adjust the loop gain of the oscillator. Figure 4.3.3(a) shows the use of a small incandescent lamp, whose resistance characteristic is shown in Figure 4.3.3(b). When the filament of the lamp is code, the resistance is small and the gain A is large. But when the lamp filament becomes hot, the resistance becomes larger and the gain A becomes small. This automatic adjustment of the gain causes distortion of the amplifier to be low and stabilizes the oscillator.

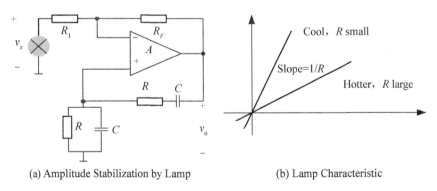

(a) Amplitude Stabilization by Lamp (b) Lamp Characteristic

Figure 4.3.3 Stabilization of a Wien-bridge Oscillator

EXAMPLE 2   Designing the Wien-bridge oscillator in Figure 4.3.1 so that $f_0 = 1\text{kHz}$

SOLUTION   The following steps can be used to complete the design.

Step1. Choose a suitable value of C: Let $C = 0.01\mu F$.

Step 2: Calculate the value of R from Equation (4.3.5):

$$R = \frac{1}{2\pi f_0 C} = \frac{1}{2\pi \times 1\text{kHz} \times 0.01\mu F} = 15915\Omega$$

Choose $R = 16\text{k}\Omega$.

Step3: Choose the value of R_F from Equation (4.3.6). Letting $R_1 = 10\text{k}\Omega$, we have

$$R_F = 2R_1 = 2 \times 10\text{k}\Omega$$

4.4 Colpitts Oscillators

A Colpitts oscillator is a tuned LC-type oscillator, as shown in Fig 4.4.1(a). LC oscillators have the advantage of having relatively small reactive elements. They exhibit higher Q than RC oscillators, but they are difficult to tune over a wide range. For a positive feedback circuit to operate as an oscillator, the loop gain must be zero. That is

$$1 - AF = 0$$

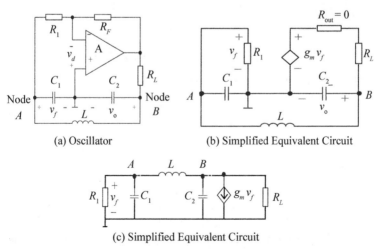

Figure 4.4.1   Colpitts Oscillator

which is really the characteristic equation of the circuit. Therefore, the condition for oscillation can be found from the characteristic equation without deriving the transfer function. Nodal analysis can be applied to find the determinant, which is then set to zero.

The op-amp operates as an inverting amplifier of the gain $A = R_F/R_1$. If the amplifier is replaced by its equivalent circuit, Figure 4.4.1(a) can be simplified to Figure 4.4.1(b). If the voltage source Av_f is replaced by its equivalent current source $g_m v_f$, Figure 4.4.1(b) can be reduced to Figure 4.4.1(c). Using nodal analysis at node B node A in Figure 4.4.1(c) gives

$$\left[sC_2 + \frac{1}{R_L} + \frac{1}{sL}\right]V_o(s) + \left[g_m - \frac{1}{sL}\right]V_f(s) = 0 \qquad (4.4.1)$$

$$-\frac{1}{sL}V_o(s) + \left[sC_1 + \frac{1}{sL} + \frac{1}{R_1}\right]V_f(s) = 0 \qquad (4.4.2)$$

To find the condition for oscillation, we set the determinant to zero,

$$\left(sC_2 + \frac{1}{R_L} + \frac{1}{sL}\right)\left(sC_1 + \frac{1}{sL} + \frac{1}{R_1}\right) + \left(g_m - \frac{1}{sL}\right)\frac{1}{sL} = 0$$

Making rearrangement yields

$$s^3 C_1 C_2 L R_1 R_L + s^2 L(C_1 R_1 + C_2 R_L) + s(C_1 R_1 R_L + C_2 R_1 R_L + L) + (R_1 + R_L + g_m R_1 R_L) = 0 \qquad (4.4.3)$$

where $g_m = \dfrac{A}{R_L} = \dfrac{R_F}{(R_1 R_L)}$. Substituting $s = j\omega$ and letting the imaginary parts equal zero, gives

$$-j\omega^3(C_1 C_2 L R_1 R_L) + j\omega(C_1 R_1 R_L + C_2 R_1 R_L + L) = 0$$

which gives the frequency of oscillation ω_0 (in rad/s) as

$$\omega_0 = \left[\frac{C_1 + C_2}{C_1 C_2 L} + \frac{1}{C_1 C_2 R_1 R_L}\right]^{\frac{1}{2}} \qquad (4.4.4)$$

Assuming that R_L is large, such that $R_1 R_L > 1/(C_1 C_2)$, Equation (4.4.4) can be approximated as

$$\omega_0 = \left[\frac{C_1 + C_2}{C_1 C_2 L}\right]^{\frac{1}{2}} \qquad (4.4.5)$$

Similarly, letting the real parts of Equation (4.4.3) equal zero yields

$$-\omega^2 L(C_1 R_1 + C_2 R_L) + (R_1 + R_L + g_m R_1 R_L) = 0$$

which gives
$$\omega^2 L(C_1 R_1 + C_2 R_L) = (R_1 + R_L + g_m R_1 R_L)$$
Substituting the value of $\omega = \omega_0$ from Equation (4.4.4) gives
$$L(C_1 R_1 + C_2 R_L) \left[\frac{C_1 + C_2}{C_1 C_2 L} + \frac{1}{C_1 C_2 R_1 R_L} \right] = (R_1 + R_L + g_m R_1 R_L)$$
After simplification, the above equation becomes
$$g_m R_1 \approx \frac{C_2}{C_1} + \frac{C_1 R_1}{C_2 R_L} + \frac{L}{C_2 R_L^2} + \frac{L}{C_1 R_1 R_L}$$
which, for a large value of R_L, becomes
$$g_m R_1 = \frac{C_2}{C_1} \qquad (4.4.6)$$

or

$$\frac{A R_1}{R_L} = \frac{R_F R_1}{R_1 R_L} = \frac{C_2}{C_1}$$

That is,

$$\frac{R_F}{R_L} = \frac{C_2}{C_1} \qquad (4.4.7)$$

which is independent of R_1 and gives the relationship among R_L, R_F, C_1, and C_2. Equation (4.4.6) gives the minimum value of $g_m \left(\text{or } \frac{R_F}{R_1 R_L} \right)$ required to sustain the oscillation with a constant amplitude. If g_m is smaller than this value, the oscillation will decay exponentially to zero. On the other hand, if g_m is larger than this value, the amplitude will rise exponentially until the nonlinearity of the op-amp limits the amplitude. Therefore, in order to ensure oscillation, the value of g_m must exceed the minimum value.

In the above analysis we use a simple op-amp model and neglecte the loss in the resistance of the inductor. As a result, we obtained relatively simple expressions for the frequency and the condition to sustain oscillation. If a complex op-amp model including the inductor loss were used, the oscillation frequency would depend (generally only slightly) on other circuit parameters. Usually, the inductor or one of the capacitors is made adjustable so that the frequency can be initially tuned to the desired value.

EXAMPLE 3   Finding the oscillation frequency of a Colpitts BJT oscillator.

Chapter 4 Oscillators

A Coplitts BJT oscillator is shown in Figure 4.4.2. The circuit parameters are $r_\pi = 1.1\text{k}\Omega$, $h_{fe} = 100$, $L = 1.5\text{mH}$, $C_1 = 1\text{nF}$, $C_2 = 99\text{nF}$ and $R_L = 10\text{k}\Omega$.

(a) Calculate the frequency of oscillation f_0.

(b) Check to make sure the condition for oscillation is satisfied.

(c) Calculate the value of R_2.

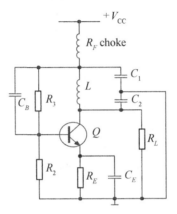

Figure 4.4.2 Colpitts BJT Oscillator

SOLUTION The *RF* choke generally has a very high impedance at the frequency of oscillation. Thus, the ac equivalent circuit is as shown in Figure 4.4.3(a). Replacing the transistor by its transconductance model (voltage-controlled current

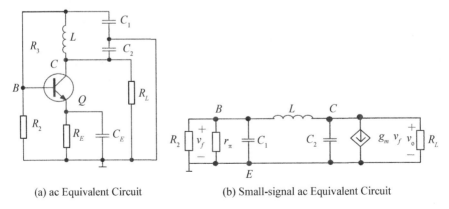

(a) ac Equivalent Circuit (b) Small-signal ac Equivalent Circuit

Figure 4.4.3 Equivalent Circuits for Example 4.3

source) gives the small-signal ac equivalent circuit shown in Figure 4.4.3(b), which is similar to the circuit shown in Figure 4.4.1(c). Thus, the analysis of the Colitts op-amp oscillator in Section 4.4 is applicable in this case:

$$g_m = h_{fe}/r_\pi = 100/1.1\text{k}\Omega = 90.91 \text{mA/V}$$

(a) From Equation (4.4.5), the frequency of oscillation is

$$f_0 = \frac{1}{2\pi}\left(\frac{C_1+C_2}{C_1 C_2 L}\right)^{\frac{1}{2}} = \frac{1}{2\pi}\left(\frac{1\text{nF}+99\text{nF}}{1\text{nF}\times 99\text{nF}\times 1.5\text{mH}}\right)^{\frac{1}{2}} = 130.6\text{kHz}$$

(b) For $R_2 \gg r_\pi$, $R_1 = r_\pi // R_2 \approx r_\pi = h_{fe}/g_m$. Therefore, Equation (4.4.6) becomes

$$g_m R_1 \approx g_m r_\pi = g_m h_{fe}/g_m = \frac{C_2}{C_1}$$

which gives

$$h_{fe} = \frac{C_2}{C_1} = \frac{99}{1} = 99$$

This value is approximately equal to the value of transistor $h_{fe} = 100$. Thus, the condition for oscillation is satisfied

(c) From Equation (4.4.6)

$$R_1 = \frac{C_2}{C_1 g_m} = 99/g_m = 99\frac{r_\pi}{h_{fe}} = 99\times 1.1\text{k}\Omega = 1089\Omega$$

Since $R_1 = r_\pi // R_2 = 1089\Omega$,

$$R_2 = 108.9\text{k}\Omega$$

4.5 Hartley Oscillators

If the inductor and the capacitors of a Colpitts op-amp oscillator are interchanged, it becomes a Hartley op-amp oscillator, as shown in Figure 4.5.1 (a). Since inductors are more expensive than capacitors, this oscillator is less desirable than a Colpitts oscillator. Replacing the amplifier with its equivalent current source reduces Figure 4.5.1(a) to Figure 4.5.1(b).

Using nodal analysis at node B and node A Figure 4.5.1(b) gives

$$\left[sC+\frac{1}{R_L}+\frac{1}{sL_2}\right]V_o(s)+(g_m-sC)V_f(s) = 0 \qquad (4.5.1)$$

Chapter 4 Oscillators

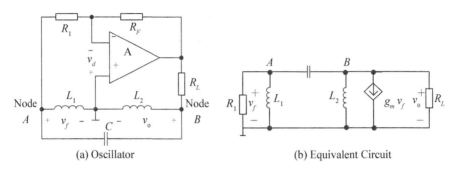

(a) Oscillator (b) Equivalent Circuit

Figure 4.5.1 Hartley Oscillator

$$-sCV_o(s) + \left[sC + \frac{1}{sL_1} + \frac{1}{R_1}\right]V_f(s) = 0 \quad (4.5.2)$$

To find the condition for oscillation, we set the determinant to zero.

$$\left(sC + \frac{1}{R_L} + \frac{1}{sL_2}\right)\left(sC + \frac{1}{sL_1} + \frac{1}{R_1}\right) + (g_m - sC)sC = 0$$

simplying the above equation gives

$$s^3 CL_1L_2(R_1 + R_L + g_m R_1 R_L) + s^2[CR_1R_L(L_1 + L_2) + L_1L_2] + s(L_1R_L + L_2R_1) + R_1R_L = 0 \quad (4.5.3)$$

where $g_m = \dfrac{A}{R_L} = \dfrac{R_F}{R_1 R_L}$. Substituting $s = j\omega$ and letting the real parts of Equation (4.5.3) equal zero, gives

$$-\omega^2[CR_1R_L(L_1 + L_2) + L_1L_2] + R_1R_L = 0$$

which gives the frequency of oscillation ω_0 as

$$\omega_0 = \frac{1}{\left[C(L_1 + L_2) + \dfrac{L_1L_2}{R_1R_L}\right]^{\frac{1}{2}}} \quad \text{(in rad/s)} \quad (4.5.4)$$

For $C(L_1 + L_2) \gg L_1L_2/R_1R_L$, Equation (4.5.3) can be approximated as

$$f_0 = \frac{1}{2\pi}\left[\frac{1}{C(L_1 + L_2)}\right]^{\frac{1}{2}} \quad \text{(in Hz)} \quad (4.5.5)$$

Letting the imaginary parts of Equation (4.5.3) equal zero, gives

$$-j\omega^3 CL_1L_2(R_1 + R_L + g_m R_1 R_L) + j\omega(L_1R_L + L_2R_1) = 0$$

Substituting $\omega = 2\pi f_0$ into Equation (4.5.5), we get

$$\frac{1}{C(L_1+L_2)}CL_1L_2(R_1+R_L+g_mR_1R_L) = L_1R_L+L_2R_1$$

which, solved for g_mR_1, gives

$$g_mR_1 = \frac{L_1}{L_2} + \frac{R_1L_2}{R_LL_1} \quad (4.5.6)$$

For a large value of R_L, Equation (4.5.6) gives the approximate value of g_m:

$$g_m \approx \frac{L_1}{R_1L_2} \quad (4.5.7)$$

Equation (4.5.7) gives the minimum value of g_m required to sustain the oscillation with a constant amplitude. To ensure oscillation, the value of g_m must exceed the minimum value. The capacitor or one of the inductors is usually made adjustable so that the frequency can be initially trimmed to the desired value.

EXAMPLE 4 Design the Hartley oscillator shown in Figure 4.5.2(a) so that $f_0 = 5\text{MHz}$. Use a n-channel JFET whose parameters are $I_{DSS} = 2 \sim 10\text{mA}$, $V_P = -6\text{V}$, and $g_m = 3 \sim 6.5\text{mA/V}$. The load resistance is $R = 100\Omega$. The power supply voltage is $V_{DD} = 15\text{V}$.

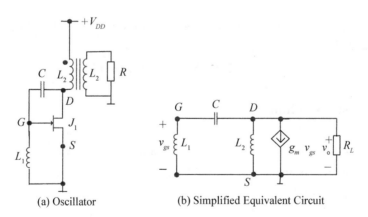

(a) Oscillator   (b) Simplified Equivalent Circuit

Figure 4.5.2 Hartley JFET Oscillator

SOLUTION The small-signal ac equivalent circuit is shown in Figure 4.5.2 (b). To ensure oscillation, we will use the minimum value of $g_m = 3\text{mA/V}$.

Step 1: Choose suitable values of L_1 and L_2: let $L_1 = L_2 = 10\mu\text{H}$

Step 2: Calculate the value of C from Equation (4.5.5):

$$C = \frac{1}{4\pi^2 f_0^2 (L_1 + L_2)} = \frac{1}{4\pi^2 \times (5\text{MHz})^2 (10\mu\text{H} + 10\mu\text{H})} = 50.66\text{pF}$$

Step 3: Find the value of effective load resistance R_L. The Q-point of the circuit is $V_{DSQ} = V_{DD} = 15\text{V}$, and $V_{GSQ} = 0$. The value of g_m varies from 3 mA/V to 6.5 mA/V. To ensure oscillation, we choose $g_m = 3$. Since R_1 is infinity in Figure 4.5.2(b), Equation (4.5.6) can be reduced to

$$g_m = \frac{L_1}{L_2 R_1} + \frac{L_2}{R_L L_1} = \frac{L_2}{R_L L_1}$$

which gives the value of effective load resistance R_L as

$$R_L = \frac{L_2}{g_m L_1} = \frac{10\mu\text{H}}{3\text{mA/V} \times 10\mu\text{H}} = 333.3\Omega$$

This is the lowest value of R_L at which sustained oscillation can occur for $g_m = 3\text{mA/V}$. Therefore, we select a higher value—say, $R_L = 400\Omega$.

Step 4: Calculate the value of turns ratio n, which is related to the load resistance R and the effective load resistance R_L by

$$n = \sqrt{\frac{R}{R_L}} = \sqrt{\frac{100}{400}} = 0.5$$

Step 5: Calculate the inductance of the transformer secondary L_3, which is related to L_2 by

$$L_3 = n^2 L_2 = 0.5^2 \times 10\mu\text{H} = 2.5\mu\text{H}$$

4.6 Crystal Oscillators

Because of their excellent frequency stability, quartz crystals are commonly used to control the frequency of oscillation. If the inductor L of the Colpitts oscillator in Figure 4.4.1(a) is changed to a crystal, the oscillator is called a crystal oscillator. Crystal oscillators are commonly used in digital signal processing. The symbol for a vibrating piezoelectric crystal is shown in Figure 4.6.1(a); its circuit model is shown in Figure 4.6.1(b), which can be simplified to Figure 4.6.1(c). The quality factor Q of a crystal can be as high as several hundred thousand. C_p represents the electrostatic capacitance between the two parallel plates of the crystal. L has a large value (as high as hundreds of heries) and is determined from $L \approx 1/C_s \omega_0^2$, where ω_0 is the resonant frequency of the crystal. R_s

4.6 Crystal Oscillators

can be as high as a few hundred thousand ohms and is determined from $R_s \approx \omega_0 L / Q$, where the quality factor Q is in the range of $10^4 \sim 10^6$. Typical values for a 2 MHz quartz crystal are $Q = 80 \times 10^3$, $C_P/C_S = 350$, $L = 520\text{mH}$, $C_S = 0.0122\text{pF}$, and $R_S = 82\Omega$.

Since Q is very high in the typical quartz crystal, we may neglect R_s. The crystal impedance is given by

$$Z(s) = \frac{1}{sC_P + sL + 1/sC_S} = \frac{1}{sC_P s^2 + (C_P + C_S)/(LC_S C_P)} = \frac{1}{sC_P} \frac{s^2 + 1/LC_S}{s^2 + \omega_p^2} \frac{s^2 + \omega_s^2}{s^2 + \omega_p^2} \quad (4.6.1)$$

If we substitute $s = j\omega$, the impedance in Equation (4.6.1) becomes

$$Z(j\omega) = -\frac{1}{\omega C_P} \frac{\omega^2 - \omega_s^2}{\omega^2 - \omega_p^2} \quad (4.6.2)$$

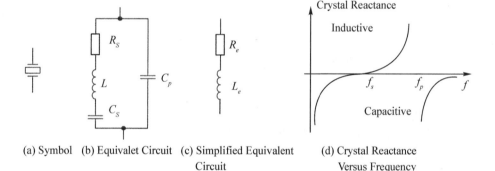

(a) Symbol (b) Equivalet Circuit (c) Simplified Equivalent Circuit (d) Crystal Reactance Versus Frequency

Figure 4.6.1 Symbol and Circuit Model of Piezoelectric Crystal

Therefore the crystal exhibits two resonant frequencies: series resonance at

$$\omega_s = \frac{1}{\sqrt{LC_s}} \quad (4.6.3)$$

and parallel resonance at

$$\omega_p = \left(\frac{C_s + C_p}{C_s C_p L}\right)^{\frac{1}{2}} \quad (4.6.4)$$

Note that $\omega_p > \omega_s$. However, since $C_p \gg C_s$, the two resonance frequencies are very close. The plot of crystal reactance against frequency in Figure 4.6.1(d) illustrates that the crystal exhibits the characteristic of an inductor over the narrow frequency range between ω_s and ω_p.

Between the resonant frequencies ω_s and ω_p, the crystal reactance is inductive, so that crystal can be substituted for an inductance, such as that in a Colpitts oscillator. Figure 4.6.2 shows a Colpitts-derived op-amp crystal oscillator, which is similar to the Colpitts oscillator in Figure 4.4.1, but with the inductor replaced by the crystal. Since the crystal reactance is inductive over a very narrow frequency range, the frequency of oscillation also confined to this narrow range and is quite constant relative to changes in bias current or temperature. Crystal oscillator frequencies are usually in the range of tens of kHz to tens of MHz.

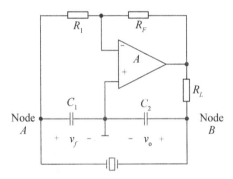

Figure 4.6.2 Crystal oscillator

The design of a sinusoidal oscillator involves the following steps:

Step 1: Identify the specifications of the output stage—for example, oscillation frequency f_0, load resistance R_L, and the dc supply voltages V_{CC} and V_{EE} (or V_{DD} and V_{SS}).

Step 2: Select the type of oscillator and the circuit topology, depending on the oscillation frequency and the types of devices availalbe, such as BJTs, MOSFET, or op-amps.

Step 3: Analyze the circuit, and find the component values such that the condition $1\angle 0°$ or $\angle 360°$ is satisfied.

Step 4: Limit the output voltage by introducing nonlinearity to stabilize the oscillator, if necessary.

Summary

Oscillators use positive feedback and are commonly employed in electronics circuits. There are many types of oscillators. However, RC, LC, and crystal oscillators are the most commonly used. For a feedback circuit to operate as an oscillator, the magnitude and the phase shift of the loop gain must be unity and 0° (or 360°), respectively. Frequency stability is an important criterion in defining the quality of an oscillator. Crystal oscillators have the highest frequency stability.

Problems

1. For the circuit in Figure p4.1, determine the values of A and θ that will produce a steady-state sinusoidal oscillation.

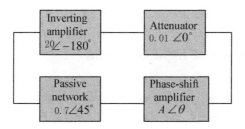

Figure p4.1

2. Design a Wien-bridge oscillator as shown in Figure 4.3.2 so that $f_0 = 5\text{kHz}$.

3. Design a Colpitts oscillator as shown in Figure 4.4.1 so that the oscillation frequency is $f_0 = 500\text{kHz}$.

4. Design a Hartley oscillator as shown in Figure 4.5.2 so that $f_0 = 500\text{kHz}$.

Chapter 5

Operational Amplifiers

We know from Chapter 2 that transistors can be used to provide amplified signals. The operational amplifier (or op-amp) is a high-gain, direct-coupled amplifier consisting of multiple stages: an input stage to provide a high input resistance with a certain amount of voltage gain, a middle stage to provide a high voltage gain, and an output stage to provide a low output resistance. It operates with a differential voltage between two input terminals, and it is a complete, integrated circuit, prepackaged amplifier. An op-amp, often referred to as a linear (or analog) integrated circuit (IC), is a very popular and versatile integrated circuit. It serves as a building block for many electronic circuits.

5.1 Characteristics of Ideal Op-Amps

The symbol for an op-amp is shown in Figure 5.1.1 (a). An op-amp has at least five terminals. Terminal 2 is called the "inverting input" because the polarity of output that results from input at this terminal will be reversed. Terminal 3 is called the "noninverting input" because the output at this terminal will have the

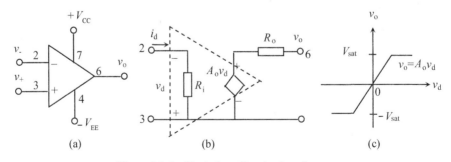

Figure 5.1.1 Equivalent Circuit of an Op-amp

same polarity as the input. Terminal 4 is for negative DC supply V_{EE}. Terminal 6 is the output terminal. Terminal 7 is for positive DC supply V_{CC}.

The output voltage of an opamp is directly proportional to the smallsignal differential (or difference) input voltage. Thus, an opamp can be modeled as a voltage-controlled voltage source; its equivalent circuit is shown in Figure 5.1.1 (b). The output voltage v_o is given by

$$v_o = A_o v_d = A_o (v_+ - v_-) \quad (5.1.1)$$

where, A_o = small signal open-loop voltage gain;

v_d = small signal differential (or difference) input voltage;

v_- = small signal voltage at the inverting terminal with respect to the ground;

v_+ = small signal voltage at the noninverting terminal with respect to the ground.

The input resistance R_i is the equivalent resistance between the differential input terminals. The input resistance of an opamp with a BJT input stage is very high, with a typical value of 2MΩ. The opamps with an FET input stage have much higher input resistances (i.e., 10^{12} Ω). Therefore, the input current drawn by the amplifier is very small (typically on the order of nA), tending to zero.

The output resistance R_o is the thevenin equivalent resistance. It is usually in the range of 10~100Ω, with a typical value of 75Ω. Its effective value is reduced, however, if external connections are made, then R_o can be neglected for most applications.

The open-loop differential voltage gain A_o is the differential voltage gain of the amplifier with no external components. It ranges from 10^4 to 10^6, with a typical value of 2×10^5. Since the value of A_o is very large. v_d becomes very small (typically on the order of μV), tending to zero. The transfer characteristic (v_o versus v_d) is shown in Figure 5.1.1(c). In reality, the output voltage cannot exceed the positive or negative saturation voltage $\pm V_{sat}$ of the op-amp, which is set by supply voltages V_{CC} and V_{EE}, respectively. The saturation voltage is usually 1V lower than the supply voltage V_{CC} or V_{EE}. Thus, the output voltage will be directly proportional to the differential input voltage v_d only until it reaches the saturation voltage; therefore the output voltage remains constant. The gain of practical opamps is also frequency dependent. The typical value of the cut-off frequency f_o is 10 Hz, with a typical gain bandwidth of 1MHz. Note that the model in Figure 5.1.1(a) does not take into account the saturation effect and assumes that gain A_o remains constant for all frequencies.

The analysis and design of circuits with op-amps can be greatly simplified if the op-amps in the circuit are assumed to be ideal. Such an assumption allows you to approximate the behavior of the op-amp circuit and to obtain the approximate values of circuit components that will satisfy some design specifications. Although the characteristics of practical op-amps differ from ideal characteristics, the errors introduced by deviations from the ideal conditions are acceptable in most applications. A complex op-amp model is used in applications requiring precise results. The circuit model of an ideal op-amp is shown in Figure 5.1.2; its characteristics are as follows:

The open-loop voltage gain is infinite: $A_o = \infty$

The input resistance is infinite: $R_i = \infty$

The output resistance is negligible: $R_o = 0$

The gain A_o remains constant and is not a function of frequency

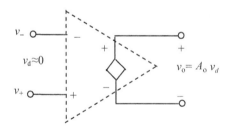

Figure 5.1.2 Model of an Ideal Op-amp

So we can draw two important conclusions:

a. Because of $R_i = \infty$, v_i is a certain value, then $i_d = 0$ — virtually open-circuited.

b. Because of $A_v = \infty$, v_o is a certain value, then $v_d = 0$, i.e., $v_+ = v_-$ — virtually short-circuited.

These are two important conclusions for us to analyze circuits with op-amp.

5.2 Analysis of Circuits with Ideal Op-Amp

In Equation (4.1) there are three possible conditions for the output voltage v_o: (a) if $v_- = 0$, v_o will be positive ($v_o = A_o v_+$), (b) if $v_+ = 0$, v_o will be negative ($v_o = -A_o v_-$), (c) if both v_+ and v_- are present, $v_o = A_o(v_+ - v_-)$. Therefore, depending on the conditions of the input voltage, opamp circuits with an op-amp can be classified into three basic configurations: inverting amplifier, noninverting amplifier, or differential (or difference) amplifier.

5.2.1 Inverting Amplifier

The configuration of an inverting amplifier is shown in Figure 5.2.1. The input voltage v_i is connected to the inverting terminal. So it is called inverting amplifier. R_f is a feedback resistor. The type of feedback is negative parallel voltage negative feedback.

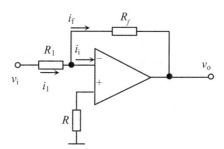

Figure 5.2.1   The Inverting Amplifiers

Using $i_d = 0$, we get

$$i_1 = i_f \quad \text{or} \quad \frac{v_i - v_-}{R_1} = \frac{v_- - v_o}{R_f} \tag{5.2.1}$$

For $v_- = v_+ = 0$, Equation (5.2.1) becomes $\dfrac{v_i}{R_1} = \dfrac{-v_o}{R_f}$

Therefore, the output voltage is related to the input voltage by

$$v_o = -\frac{R_f}{R_1} v_i \tag{5.2.2}$$

The closed-loop voltage gain is

$$A_V = -\frac{R_f}{R_1}$$

The significance of this result is that the terminal voltage gain, the usable voltage gain, is independent of the parameters of the amplifier, and depends only on the external components R_1 and R_f.

Since $v_d = 0$, the effective input resistance R_{in} of the amplifier is given by $R_{in} = R_1$. The effective output resistance is given by $R_{out} = 0$.

5.2.2 Noninverting Amplifier

The configuration of an inverting amplifier is shown in Figure 5.2.2(a). The input voltage v_i is applied directly at the noninverting terminal. So it is called noninverting amplifier. R_f is a feedback resistor. The type of feedback is negative series voltage negative feedback.

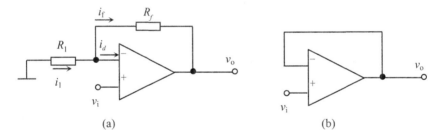

Figure 5.2.2 The Noninverting Amplifiers

Using $v_+ = v_- = v_i$ and $i_d = 0$ we get $i_1 = i_f$, that is,

$$\frac{0 - v_-}{R_1} = \frac{v_- - v_o}{R_f} \quad \text{or} \quad \frac{v_+}{R_1} = -\frac{v_+ - v_o}{R_f}$$

simplying the above equation yields

$$v_o = \left(1 + \frac{R_f}{R_1}\right) v_+ = \left(1 + \frac{R_f}{R_1}\right) v_i \qquad (5.2.3)$$

The close-loop voltage gain A_f is

$$A_f = 1 + \frac{R_f}{R_1} \qquad (5.2.4)$$

Since the current drawn by the amplifier is zero, the effective input resistance of the amplifier is very high, tending to infinity: $R_{in} = \infty$. The effective output resistance is given by $R_{out} = 0$. If $R_f = 0$ or $R_1 = \infty$, as shown in Figure 5.2.2 (b). Equation (5.2.4) becomes

$$A_f = 1$$

That is, the output voltage equals the input voltage: $v_o = v_i$, the circuit of Figure 5.2.2 (b) is commonly referred to as a voltage follower, since its output voltage follows the input voltage. It has the inherent characteristics of a high input resistance typically $10^{10}\Omega$ and a low output typically $50m\Omega$. A voltage follower is commonly used as the buffer stage between a low impedance load and a source requiring a high resistance load.

5.2.3 Differential Amplifier

In the differential amplifiers configuration, shown in Figure 5.2.3, the two input voltages v_a and v_b are applied at the noninverting terminal and at the inverting terminal respectively. Resistance R_a and R_b are used to step down the voltage applied at the noninverting terminal. Let us apply the superposition theorem to find the output voltage v_o. that is, we will find the output voltage v_{oa}, which is due to v_a only, and then we will find the output voltage v_{ob}, which is due to v_b only. The output voltage will be the sum of v_{oa} and v_{ob}.

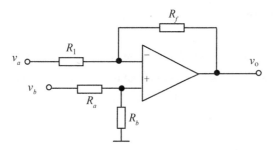

Figure 5.2.3 The Differential Amplifiers

The voltage v_+ can be related to the input voltage v_b by

$$v_+ = \frac{R_b}{R_a + R_b} v_b \qquad (5.2.5)$$

Applying Equations (5.2.4) and (5.2.5) gives the output voltage v_{ob}, which is due to the input at the noninverting terminal, as

$$v_{ob} = \left(1+\frac{R_f}{R_1}\right)v_+ = \left(\frac{R_b}{R_a+R_b}\right)\left(1+\frac{R_f}{R_1}\right)v_b$$

Applying Equation (5.2.2) gives the output voltage v_{oa}, which is due to the input at the inverting terminal, as

$$v_{oa} = -\frac{R_f}{R_1}v_a$$

Therefore, the resultant output voltage is given by

$$v_o = v_{oa}+v_{ob} = -\frac{R_f}{R_1}v_a + \left(\frac{R_b}{R_a+R_b}\right)\left(1+\frac{R_f}{R_1}\right)v_b$$

which, for $R_b = R_1$ and $R_f = R_a$, becomes

$$v_o = \frac{R_f}{R_1}(v_b-v_a) \qquad (5.2.6)$$

Thus, the circuit in Figure 5.2.3 can operate as a differential voltage amplifier with a closed-loop voltage gain of R_f/R_1. If all the resistances have the same values, Equation (5.2.6) becomes

$$v_o = v_b - v_a$$

Under this condition, the circuit will operated as a difference amplifier.

5.3 Applications

The opamps is used extensively in many devices, along with resistors and other passive elements. Most of the applications are derived from the basic op-amp configuration described in Sec.5.2. In this section we will discuss several applications of op-amps.

5.3.1 The Integrator

If the resistance R_f of the inverting amplifier of Figure 5.2.1 is replaced by a capacitance C_f, the circuit will operate as an integrator. Such a circuit is shown in Figure 5.3.1 v_o equation can also be derived from a circuit analysis similar to that discussed in Sec.5.2. That is,

$$i_1 = i_f, \quad \frac{v_i}{R_1} = C_f \frac{d(0-v_o)}{dt}$$

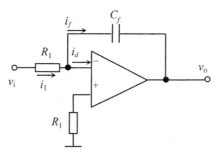

Figure 5.3.1　The integrator

so
$$v_o(t) = -\frac{1}{R_f C_f} \int_0^t v_i(t)\,dt$$

5.3.2　The Differentiator

If the resistance R_1 of the inverting amplifier of Figure 5.2.1 is replaced by a capacitance C_1, the circuit will operate as a differentiator. Such a circuit is shown in Figure 5.3.2. v_o can also be derived from a circuit analysis similar to that discussed in Sec.5.2. That is,

$$i_1 = i_f$$

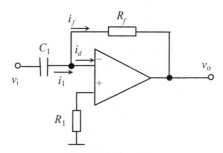

Figure 5.3.2　The differentiator

$$\frac{0-v_o}{R_f} = C_1 \frac{dv_i}{dt}$$

so
$$v_o = -R_f C_1 \frac{dv_i}{dt}$$

5.3.3 Noninverting Summing Amplifier

The basic noninverting amplifier in Figure 5.2.2 can be operated as a summing amplifier. A noninverting summing amplifier with three inputs is shown in Figure 5.3.3. Summing amplifiers are commonly used in analog computing. Applying the superposition theorem gives the voltage v_+ at the noninverting terminal

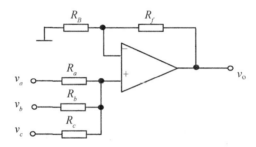

Figure 5.3.3 Noninverting Summing Amplifier

$$v_+ = \frac{R_b // R_c}{R_a + R_b // R_c} v_a + \frac{R_a // R_c}{R_b + R_a // R_c} v_b + \frac{R_b // R_a}{R_c + R_b // R_a} v_c$$

$$= \frac{R_A}{R_a} v_a + \frac{R_A}{R_b} v_b + \frac{R_A}{R_c} v_c \tag{5.3.1}$$

where
$$R_A = R_a // R_b // R_c \tag{5.3.2}$$

Applying Equation (5.2.3) for the noninverting amplifier and Equation (5.3.1) gives the output voltage

$$v_o = \left(1 + \frac{R_f}{R_B}\right) v_+ = \left(1 + \frac{R_f}{R_B}\right)\left(\frac{R_A}{R_a} v_a + \frac{R_A}{R_b} v_b + \frac{R_A}{R_c} v_c\right) \tag{5.3.3}$$

for $R_a = R_b = R_b = R$, Equation (5.3.2) gives $R_A = R/3$, and Equation (5.3.3) becomes

$$v_o = \left(1 + \frac{R_f}{R_B}\right)\left(\frac{v_a + v_b + v_c}{3}\right)$$

Thus, the output is equal to the average of all the input voltages times the closed-loop gain $(1+R_f/R_B)$ of the circuit. If the circuit is operated as a unity follower with $R_f=0$ and $R_B=\infty$, the output voltage will be equal to the average of all the input voltage.

$$v_o = \frac{v_a+v_b+v_c}{3} \qquad (5.3.4)$$

If the closed-loop gain $(1+R_f/R_B)$ is made equal to the number of inputs, the output voltage becomes equal to the sum of all the input voltages. That is, for three inputs, $n=3$, and $(1+R_f/R_B)=n=3$. Then Equation (5.3.4) becomes

$$v_o = v_a+v_b+v_c$$

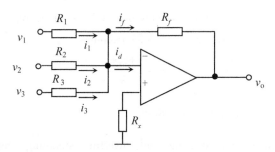

Figure 5.3.4 The Inverting Summing Amplifier

5.3.4 Inverting Summing Amplifier

The basic inverting amplifier in Figure 5.2.1 can be operated as an inverting summing amplifier. An inverting summing amplifier with three inputs is shown in Figure 5.3.4. Depending on the values of the feedback resistance R_f and the input resistance R_1, R_2, and R_3, the circuit can be operated as a summing amplifier, a scaling amplifier, or an averaging amplifier. Since the output voltage is reverted, another inverter may be required, depending on the desired polarity of the voltage.

For an ideal opamp, $v_d \approx 0$. Using Ohm's law, gives

$$i_1 = \frac{v_1}{R_1}, \quad i_2 = \frac{v_2}{R_2}, \quad i_3 = \frac{v_3}{R_3}, \quad i_f = -\frac{v_o}{R_f}$$

Since the current entering the opamp is zero ($i_d=0$),

or

$$i_1+i_2+i_3 = i_f$$

$$\frac{v_1}{R_1}+\frac{v_2}{R_2}+\frac{v_3}{R_3} = -\frac{v_o}{R_f}$$

which gives the output voltage as

$$v_o = -\left(\frac{R_f}{R_1}v_1+\frac{R_f}{R_2}v_2+\frac{R_f}{R_3}v_3\right) \qquad (5.3.5)$$

Thus, v_o is weighted sum of the input voltages, and this circuit is also called a weighted, or scaling, summer. If $R_1 = R_2 = R_3 = R_f = R$, Equation (5.3.5) becomes

$$v_o = -(v_1+v_2+v_3)$$

and the circuit is called a summing amplifier. If $R_1 = R_2 = R_3 = nR_f$, where n is the number of input signals and the circuit operates as an averaging amplifier. For three inputs, $n=3$, and Equation (5.3.5) becomes

$$v_o = -\frac{v_1+v_2+v_3}{3}$$

5.3.5 Addition-Subtraction Amplifier

The function of noninverting and inverting summing amplifiers can be implemented by only one opamp, as shown in Figure 5.3.5. The output voltage is

$$v_o = A_1v_a+A_2v_b+A_3v_c-B_1v_1-B_2v_2-B_3v_3$$

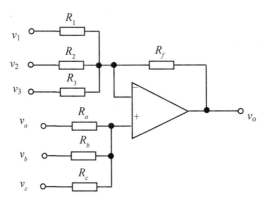

Figure 5.3.5 The Addition-Subtraction Amplifier

where A_1, A_2, A_3, B_1, B_2, and B_3 are the gain constants. Applying Equations (5.3.3) and (5.3.5) gives an expression for the resultant output voltage:

$$v_o = \left(1 + \frac{R_f}{R_B}\right)\left(\frac{R_A}{R_a}v_a + \frac{R_A}{R_b}v_b + \frac{R_A}{R_c}v_c\right) - \left(\frac{R_f}{R_1}v_1 + \frac{R_f}{R_2}v_2 + \frac{R_f}{R_3}v_3\right) \quad (5.3.6)$$

where $\quad R_A = R_a // R_b // R_c, \quad R_B = R_1 // R_2 // R_3$

5.4 Active Filters

A popular application uses opamps to build active filter circuits. A filter circuit can be constructed using passive components: resistors and capacitors. An active filter additionally uses an amplifier to provide voltage amplification and signal isolation or buffering.

A filter that provides a constant output from dc up to a cutoff frequency f_{OH} and then passes no signal above that frequency is called an ideal low-pass filter. The ideal response of a low-pass filter is shown in Figure 5.4.1(a). A filter that provides or passes signals above a cutoff frequency f_{OL} is a high-pass filter, as idealized in Figure 5.4.1(b). When the filter circuit passes signals that are above one ideal cutoff frequency and below a second cutoff frequency, it is called a bandpass filter, as idealized in Figure 5.4.1(c).

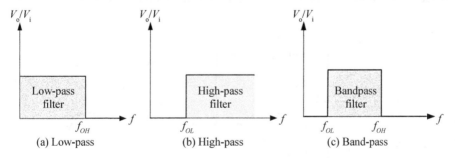

Figure 5.4.1 Ideal Filter Responses

5.4.1 Low-Pass Filter

A first-order, low-pass filter using a single resistor and capacitor as shown in

Figure 5.4.2(a) has a practical slope of -20dB per decade, as shown in Figure 5.4.2(b) (rather than the ideal response of Figure 5.4.1(a)). The voltage gain is

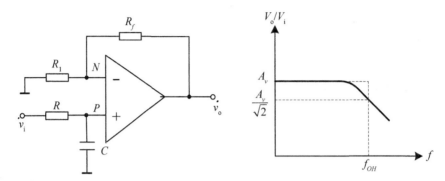

Figure 5.4.2   First-order Low-pass Active Filter

$$A_v = 1 + \frac{R_f}{R_1} \tag{5.4.1}$$

the cutoff frequency is

$$f_{OH} = \frac{1}{2\pi RC} \tag{5.4.2}$$

Connecting two sections of filters as shown in Figure 5.4.3 results in a second-order low-pass filter with cutoff at $-$ 40dB per decade $-$ close to the ideal characteristic of Figure 5.4.3(a). The voltage gain and the cutoff frequency are the

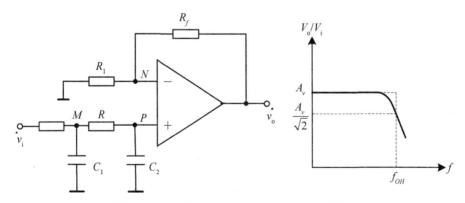

Figure 5.4.3   Second-order Low-pass Active Filter

same for the second-order circuit as for the first-order filter circuit, except that the filter response drops at a faster rate for a second-order filter circuit.

5.4.2 High-pass Active Filter

First and second order high-pass active filters can be built as shown in Figure 5.4.4. The amplifier gain is calculated using Equation 11.8. The cutoff frequency is

$$f_{OL} = \frac{1}{2\pi RC}$$

A second-order filter results in the same cutoff frequency as shown in Equation 5.4.2.

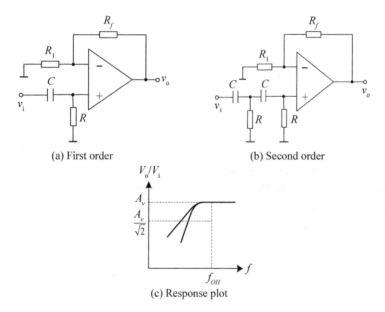

Figure 5.4.4 High-pass Filters

5.4.3 Bandpass Filter

Figure 5.4.5 shows a bandpass filter with two stages. The first stage is a high-pass filter and second a low-pass filter. The combination of them form a bandpass filter.

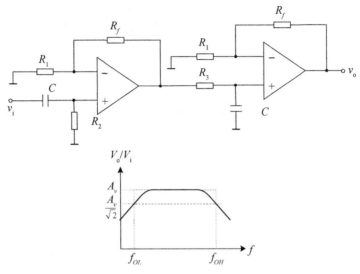

Figure 5.4.5 Bandpass Active Filter

5.5 Comparator

The comparator is essentially an opamp operated in an open-loop configuration, as shown in Figure 5.5.1(a). As the name implies, a comparator compares two voltages to determine which is larger. The comparator is usually biased as voltages $+V_S$ and $-V_S$, although other biases are possible.

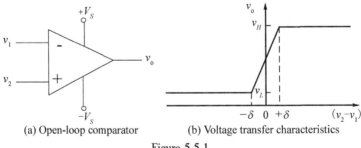

(a) Open-loop comparator   (b) Voltage transfer characteristics

Figure 5.5.1

The voltage transfer characteristics, neglecting any offset voltage effects, are shown in Figure 5.5.1(b). When v_2 is slightly greater than v_1, the output reaches a high saturated state V_H; When v_2 is slightly less than v_1, the output reaches a low saturated state V_L; The saturated output voltages V_H and V_L may be close to the supply voltages $+V_S$ and $-V_S$, respectively, which means that V_L may be negative. The transition region is the region in which the output voltage is in neither of its saturation states. This region occurs when the differential input voltage is in the range $-\delta < (v_2 - v_1) < +\delta$. If, for example, the open-loop gain is 10^5 and the difference between the two output states is $(V_H - V_L) = 10V$, then

$$2\delta = 10/10^5 = 10^{-4} V = 0.1 mV$$

The range of differential input voltage in the transition region is normally very small.

One major difference between a comparator and opamp is that a comparator need not be frequency compensated. Frequency stability is not a consideration since the comparator reaches one of two states. Since a comparator does not contain a frequency compensation capacitor, it is not slew-rate-limited by the compensation capacitor as is the op-amp. Typical response time for the comparator output to change states are in the range of 30~200ns. An expected response time for a 741 op-amp with a slew rate of $0.7V/\mu s$ is on the order of $30\mu s$, which is a factor of 1000 times greater.

Figure 5.5.2 shows two comparator configurations along with their voltage transfer characteristics. In both, the input transition region width is assumed to be negligibly small. The reference voltage may be either positive or negative, and the output saturation voltages are assumed to be symmetrical about zero. The crossover voltage is defined as input voltage at which the output changes states.

Two other comparator configurations, in which the crossover voltage is a function of resistor ratios, are shown in Figure 5.5.3. Input bias current compensation is also included in this figure. In Figure 5.5.3(a), we use the superposition principle to obtain

$$v_+ = \left(\frac{R_2}{R_1 + R_2}\right) V_{REF} + \left(\frac{R_1}{R_1 + R_2}\right) v_I \qquad (5.5.1)$$

The ideal crossover voltage occurs when $v_+ = 0$ or

$$R_2 V_{REF} + R_1 v_I = 0$$

which can be written as

$$v_I = -\frac{R_2}{R_1} V_{REF}$$

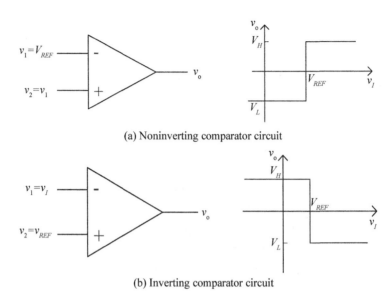

(a) Noninverting comparator circuit

(b) Inverting comparator circuit

Figure 5.5.2

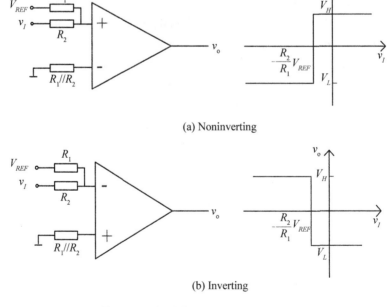

(a) Noninverting

(b) Inverting

Figure 5.5.3 Other comparator circuits

The output goes high when $v_+ > 0$. From Equation (5.5.1), we see that v_o is High when v_I is greater than the crossover voltage. A similar analysis produces the characteristics shown in Figure 5.5.3(b).

5.5.1 Basic Inverting Schmitt Trigger

The Schmitt trigger or bistable multivibrator uses positive feedback with a loop-gain greater than unity to produce a bistable characteristic. Figure 5.5.4(a) shows one configuration of a Schmitt trigger. Positive feedback occurs because the feedback resistor is connected between the output and noninverting input terminals. Voltage v_+, in terms of the output voltage, can be found by using a voltage divider equation to yield

$$v_+ = \left(\frac{R_1}{R_1+R_2}\right) v_o$$

The voltage v_+ does not remain constant; rather, it is a function of the output voltage. The input signal v_I is applied at the inverting terminal.

5.5.2 Voltage Transfer Characteristic

To determine the voltage transfer characteristics, we assume that the output of the comparator is in one state, namely $v_o = V_H$, which is the high state. Then

$$v_+ = \left(\frac{R_1}{R_1+R_2}\right) V_H$$

As long as the input signal is less than v_+, the output remains in its high state. The crossover voltage occurs when $v_I = v_+$ and is defined as V_{TH}. We have

$$V_{TH} = \left(\frac{R_1}{R_1+R_2}\right) V_H \qquad (5.5.2)$$

When v_I is greater than V_{TH}, the voltage at the inverting terminal is greater than that at the noninverting terminal. The differential input voltage $v_I - V_{TH}$ is amplified by the open-loop gain of the comparator, and the output switches to its low state, or $v_o = V_L$. The voltage v_+ becomes

$$v_+ = \left(\frac{R_1}{R_1+R_2}\right) V_L$$

Since $V_L < V_H$, the input voltage v_I is still greater than v_+, and the output remains in its low state as v_I continues to increase. This voltage transfer characteristic is shown in Figure 5.5.4(b). We assume that V_H is positive and V_L is negative in these transfer characteristics.

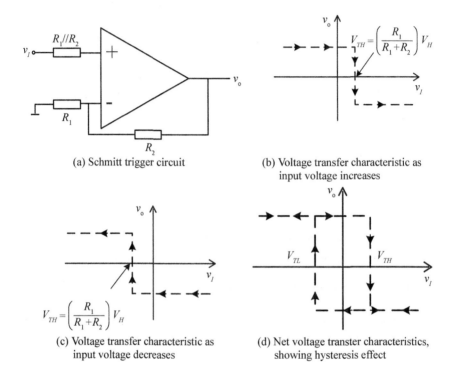

(a) Schmitt trigger circuit

(b) Voltage transfer characteristic as input voltage increases

(c) Voltage transfer characteristic as input voltage decreases

(d) Net voltage transfer characteristics, showing hysteresis effect

Figure 5.5.4

Now consider the transfer characteristic as v_I decreases. As long as v_I is larger than $v_+ = [R_1/(R_1+R_2)]V_L$, the output remains in its low saturation state. The crossover voltage now occurs when $v_I = v_+$ and is defined as V_{TL}. We have

$$V_{TL} = \left(\frac{R_1}{R_1+R_2}\right) V_L \qquad (5.5.3)$$

As v_I drops below this value, the voltage at the noninverting terminal is greater than that at the inverting terminal. The differential voltage at the comparator terminals is amplified by the open-loop gain, and the output switches to its high state, or $v_o = v_H$. As v_I continues to decrease, it remains less than v_+; therefore, v_o remains in its high state. This voltage transfer characteristic is shown in Figure 5.5.4(c).

The complete voltage transfer characteristics of the Schmitt trigger in Figure 5.5.4(a) combine the characteristics in Figure 5.5.4(b) and 5.5.4(c). These complete characteristics are shown in Figure 5.5.4(d). The crossover voltages depend on whether the input voltage increases or decreases. The complete transfer characteristics therefore show a hysteresis. The width of the hysteresis is the difference between the two crossover voltage V_{TH} and V_{TL}.

The bistable characteristic of the circuit occurs at the point $v_I = 0$, at which the output may be in either its high or low state. The output remains in either state as long as v_I remains in the range $V_{TL} < v_I < V_{TH}$. The output switches states only if the input increases above V_{TH} or decreases below V_{TL}.

EXAMPLE 5.1   Determine the hysteresis width of a particular Schmitt trigger.

Consider the Schmitt trigger in Figure 5.5.4(a), with parameters $R_1 = 10\text{k}\Omega$ and $R_2 = 90\text{k}\Omega$. Let $V_H = 10\text{V}$ and $V_L = -10\text{V}$.

SOLUTION: From Equation (5.4.2), the upper crossover voltage is

$$V_{TH} = \left(\frac{R_1}{R_1 + R_2}\right) V_H = \left(\frac{10}{10+90}\right) 10 = 1\text{V}$$

and from Equation (5.4.3), the lower crossover voltage is

$$V_{TL} = \left(\frac{R_1}{R_1 + R_2}\right) V_L = \left(\frac{10}{10+90}\right)(-10) = -1\text{V}$$

The hysteresis width is therefore $(V_{TH} - V_{TL}) = 2\text{V}$.

The complete voltage transfer characteristics in Figure 5.5.4(d) show the inverting characteristics of this particular Schmitt trigger. When the input signal becomes positive enough, the output is in its low state; when the input signal is negative enough, the output is in its high state. Since the input signal is applied at the inverting terminal of the comparator, this characteristic is as expected.

Summary

An op-amp is a high-gain differential amplifier that can be used to perform various functions in electronic circuits. Op-amps are normally used with a feedback circuit, and the output voltage becomes almost independent of the op-amp parameters. The basic configurations of op-amp amplifiers can be used in many applications such as integrators, differentiators, inductance simulators, meters, limiters, detectors and precision rectifiers.

The analysis of an op-amp circuit can be simplified by the assumption of ideal characteristics. An ideal op-amp has a very high voltage gain, a very high input resistance, a very low output resistance, and a negligible input current. The characteristics of practical op-amps differ from the ideal characteristics, but analyses based on the ideal conditions are valid for many applications and provide the starting point for practical circuit design. Although the DC model of op-amps can be used to analyze complex op-amp circuits, it does not take into account the frequency dependency and op-amp nonlinearities. If the op-amp is operated at frequencies higher than the op-amp break frequency, the effect of frequency should be evaluated.

Problems

5.1 Calculate the output voltage as in Figure p5.1 (an ideal op-amp circuit).

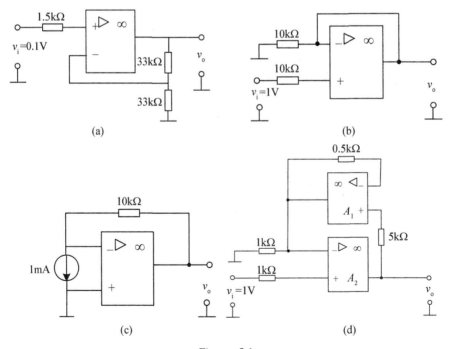

Figure p5.1

5.2 If the circuit of Figure p5.2 has $v_i = 100\sin\omega t$ mV, what output voltage vo results?

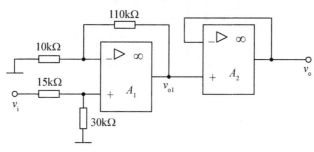

Figure p5.2

5.3 The circuit is shown in Figure p5.3, calculate the relationship between v_o and v_i in the following conditions:
(1) S_1 and S_3 are closed, S_2 is turned off.
(2) S_1 and S_2 are closed, S_3 is turned off.
(3) S_2 is closed, S_1 and S_3 are turned off.
(4) S_1, S_2, S_3 are closed.

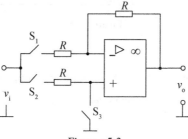

Figure p5.3

5.4 Adjustable gain inverting the ratio calculation circuit is shown in Figure p5.4, the circuit output is $V_o(\text{sat}) = \pm 15\text{v}$, $R_1 = 100\text{k}\Omega$, $R_2 = 200\text{k}\Omega$, $R_P = 5\text{k}\Omega$, $V_i = 2\text{V}$, calculate v_o in the following conditions.
(1) R_P slider at the top position.
(2) R_P slider in the middle position.
(3) R_P slider at the bottom position.

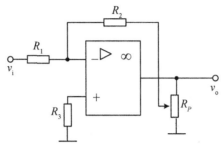

Figure 5.4

5.5 Calculate V_o in the circuit shown in Figure p5.5.

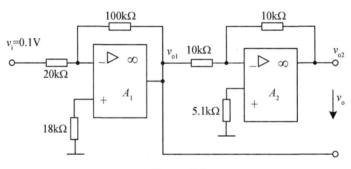

Figure p5.5

5.6 In the circuit shown in Figure p5.6, supposing that $V_C(0) = 0V$, calculate the output v_o when $t = 5$ seconds.

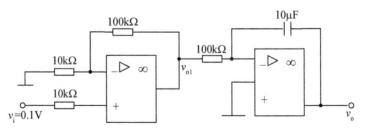

Figure p5.6

5.7 In the circuit shown in Figure p5.7, supposing that output voltage v_o = 3V, the driver alarm send out warning signal, if $v_{i1} = 1V$, $v_{i2} = -4.5V$, how much v_{i3} is when sending out warning signal?

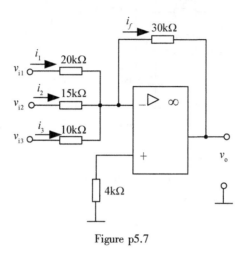

Figure p5.7

5.8 Determine the output voltage for the circuit of Figure p5.8.

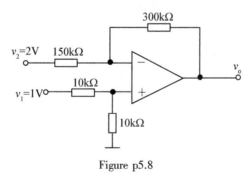

Figure p5.8

5.9 Calculate the cutoff frequency of a first-order low-pass filter in the circuit of Figure p5.9.

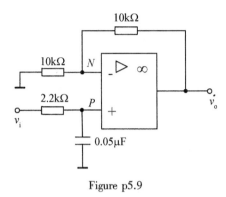

Figure p5.9

5.10 Sketch the output waveform for the circuit of Figure p5.10?

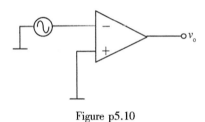

Figure p5.10

5.11 Determine the output voltage of an op-amp for input voltages of $V_{i1} = 150\mu V$, $V_{i2} = 140\mu V$. The amplifier has a differential gain of Ad and the value of CMRR is:
  a. 100
  b. 10^5

Chapter 6

Introductory Digital Concepts

6.1 Digital and Analog Quantities

An analog quantity is one having continuous values. A digital quantity is one having a discrete set of values. This is the basic difference between analog and digital quantities. Most things that can be measured quantitatively occur in nature in analog form.

Now you sample values representing the analog quantity at discrete points in time, then you have effectively converted an analog quantity to a form that can now be digitized by representing each sampled value by a digital code that consists of a series of 1s and 0s.

The Digital Advantage: Digital representation has certain advantage over analog representation in electronic applications. For one thing, digital data can be processed and transmitted more efficiently and reliably than the analog data. Also, digital data has a great advantage when the storage is necessary. For example, music when converted to digital form can be stored more compacted and reproduced with greater accuracy and clarity than is possible when it is in analog form. Noise (unwanted voltage fluctuation) does not affect digital data nearly as much as it does analog signals.

6.2 Binary Digitals, Logic Levels and Digital Waveforms

6.2.1 Binary Digits

Each of the two digits in the binary system, 1 or 0, is called a *bit*, which is a contraction of the words binary digit. In digital circuit, two different voltage levels are used to represent the two bits. Generally, 1 is represented by the higher voltage, which we will refer to as a HIGH, and a 0 is represented by the lower voltage level, which we will refer to as a LOW. This is called *positive logic* and will be used throughout the book.

$$\text{HIGH} = 1 \quad \text{and} \quad \text{LOW} = 0$$

Another system where a 1 is represented by a LOW and a 0 is represented by a HIGH is called *negative logic*.

Groups of bits (combinations of 1s and 0s), called *codes*, are used to represent numbers, letters, symbols, instructions, and anything else in a given application.

6.2.2 Logic Levels

The voltages used to represent a 1 and a 0 are called *logic levels*. Ideally, one voltage level represents a HIGH and another represents a LOW.

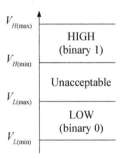

Figure 6.2.1 Logic Level Ranges of Voltage for a Digital Circuit

In a practical digital circuit, however, a HIGH can be any voltage between a specified minimum value and a specified maximum value. Likewise, a LOW can be any voltage between a specified minimum and a specified maximum. There can be no overlap between the accepted range of HIGH levels and the accepted range of LOW levels.

6.2.3 Digital Waveforms

Digital waveforms consist of voltage levels that are changing back and forth

6.2 Binary Digitals, Logic Levels and Digital Waveforms

between the HIGH and LOW levels or states. A positive-going pulse is generated when the voltage (or current) goes from its normally LOW level to its HIGH level and then back to its LOW level. A negative-going pulse is generated when the voltage (or current) goes from its normally HIGH level to its LOW level and then back to its HIGH level. A digital waveform is made up of a series of pulses.

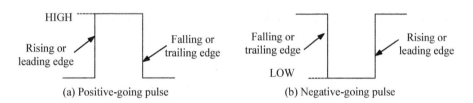

(a) Positive-going pulse   (b) Negative-going pulse

Figure 6.2.2

6.2.4 The Pulse

As indicated in Figure 6.2.3, a pulse has two edges: a leading/rising edge and a trailing/falling edge. For the ideal pulse we assume that the rising and falling edges interchange without time (instantaneously). In practice, these transitions never occur instantaneously. Figure 6.2.3 shows the various parameters of a pulse waveform.

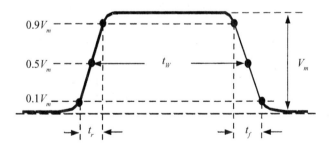

Figure 6.2.3   Nonideal Pulse Characteristics

Rise time (t_r): the time required to go from its LOW to HIGH (In practice, from 10% of the pulse amplitude to 90%)

Fall time (t_f): the time required to go from its HIGH to LOW (In practice, from 90% of the pulse amplitude to 10%)

Pulse width (t_w): the duration of the pulse (the time interval between the 50% points on the rising and falling edges)

The pulse can be classified as either periodic or nonperodic. A periodic pulse waveform is one that repeats itself at a fixed interval, called a period (T). The frequency (f) is the rate at which it repeats itself and is measured in hertz (H_z).

$$f=\frac{1}{T}, \quad T=\frac{1}{f}$$

$$\text{Duty cycle}=\left(\frac{t_w}{T}\right)100\%$$

A digital waveform with binary information: Binary information that is handled by digital systems appears as waveforms that represent sequences of bits. When the waveform is HIGH, a binary 1 is present; when the waveform is LOW, a binary 0 is present. Each bit in a sequence occupies a defined time interval called a bit time.

In digital systems, all waveforms are synchronized with a basic timing waveform called the clock.

A timing diagram is a graph of digital waveforms showing the actual time relationship of two or more waveforms and how each waveform changes in relation to the others. By looking at the timing diagram, you can determine the state (HIGH or LOW) of all the waveforms at any specified point in time and the exact time that a waveform changes state relative to the other waveforms.

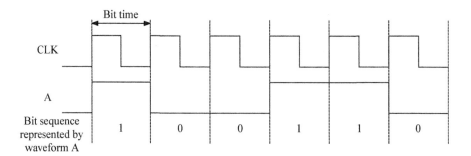

Figure 6.2.4 Example of a Clock Waveform Synchronized with a Waveform Representation of a Sequence of Bits

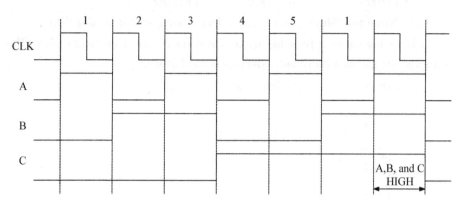

Figure 6.2.5 Example of Timing Diagram

Summary

In this chapter, the basic difference between analog and digital circuit is introduced. In digital circuit, two different voltage levels are used to represent the logical value (0 and 1). Digital waveform can be used to represent digital signal.

Problems

6.1 Choice question:
(1) A quantity having continuous values is
    (a) a digital quantity   (b) an analog quantity
    (c) a binary quantity   (d) a natural quantity
(2) The term *bit* means
    (a) a small amount of data   (b) a 1 or a 0
    (c) binary digit   (d) both answers (b) and (c)
(3) A pluse in a certain waveform occurs every 10ms. The frequency is
    (a) 1kHz   (b) 1Hz   (c) 100 Hz   (d) 10 Hz
(4) In a certain digital waveform, the period is twice the pulse width. The duty cycle is

(a) 100%   (b) 200%   (c) 50%

6.2 Name two advantages of digital data as compared to analog data.

6.3 A portion of a periodic digital waveform is shown in Figure p6.3. The measurements are in milliseconds. Determine the following:

(a) period   (b) frequency   (c) duty cycle

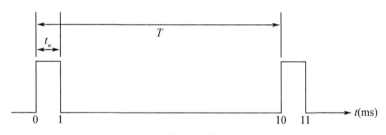

Figure p6.3

Chapter 7

Number Systems, Operations, and Codes

7.1 Binary-to-Decimal Conversion

As explained earlier, the binary number system is a positional system where each binary digit (bit) carries a certain weight based on its position relative to the binary point. Any binary number can be converted to its decimal equivalent simply by summing together the weights of the various positions in the binary number which contain a 1. Here is an example:

$$1 \quad 1 \quad 0 \quad 1 \quad 1 \quad \text{(binary)}$$
$$2^4 + 2^3 + 0 + 2^1 + 2^0 = 16+8+2+1 = 27_{10}(\text{decimal})$$

The same method is used for binary numbers that contain a fractional part:

$$101.10\ 1 = 2^2 + 2^0 + 2^{-1} + 2^{-3}$$
$$= 4+1+0.5+0.125$$
$$= 5.625_{10}$$

The following conversions should be performed and verified by the reader:

(1) $100110_2 = 38_{10}$;
(2) $0.110001_2 = 0.765625_{10}$;
(3) $11110011.0101_2 = 243.3125$.

7.2 Decimal-to-Binary Conversion

There are several ways to convert a decimal number to its equivalent binary-system representation: A method that is convenient for small numbers is the reverse of the process described in Section7.3.1 The decimal number is simply expressed as a sum of powers of 2 and then 1s and 0s are written in the appropriate bit positions. For example

$$(13)_{10} = 8+4+1 = 2^3+2^2+0+2^1$$
$$= (1\ 1\ 0\ 1)_2$$

Another example:
$$(25.375)_{10} = 16+8+1+0.25+0.125$$
$$= 2^4+2^3+0+0+2^0+0+2^{-2}+2^{-3}$$
$$= (1\ 1\ 0\ 0\ 1\ 0\ 1\ \ \ 1)_2$$

For larger decimal numbers, the above method is laborious. A more convenient method entails separate conversion of the integer and fractional parts. For example, take the decimal number 25.375 which was converted above. The first step is to convert the integer portion, 25. This conversion is accomplished by repeatedly dividing 25 by 2 and writing down the remainders after each division until a quotient of zero is obtained:

The desired binary conversion is obtained by writing down the remainders as shown above. Note that the *first* remainder is the LSB and the *last* remainder is the MSB.

$$\frac{25}{2} = 12\quad + \text{remainder of } 1$$

$$\frac{12}{2} = 6\quad + \text{remainder of } 0$$

$$\frac{6}{2} = 3\quad + \text{remainder of } 0$$

$$\frac{3}{2} = 1\quad + \text{remainder of } 1$$

$$\frac{1}{2} = 0\quad + \text{remainder of } 1$$

MSB   LSB
$$(25)_{10} = (1\quad 1\quad 0\quad 0\quad 1)_2$$

The fractional part of the number (0.375) is converted to binary by repeatedly *multiplying* it by 2 and recording any carries in the integer position:

$$0.375 \times 2 = 0.75 = 0.75 + \text{carry of } 0$$
$$0.75 \times 2 = 1.50 = 0.50 + \text{carry of } 1$$
$$0.50 \times 2 = 1.00 = 0.00 + \text{carry of } 1$$

$$(0.375)_{10} = (0.011)_2$$

Note that the repeated multiplications continue until a product of exactly 1.00 appears, since further multiplication results in all zeros. Notice here that the *first* array is written in the first position to the right of the binary point.

Finally the complete conversion for 25.375 can be written as the combination of the integer and fraction conversions:

$$(25.375)_{10} = (11001.011)_2$$

The reader should apply this method to verify the following conversion:

$$(632.85)_{10} = (1001111000.11011)_2$$

7.3 Binary Addition

The addition of two binary numbers is performed in exactly the same manner as the addition of decimal numbers. In fact, binary addition is simpler since there are fewer cases to learn. Let us first review decimal addition:

```
    3 7 6
  + 4 6 1
    8 3 7
```

The least-significant-digit (LSD) position is operated on first producing a sum of 7. The digits in the second position are then added to produce a sum of 13 which produces a carry of 1 into the third position. This produces a sum of 8 in the third position.

The same general steps are followed in binary addition. However, there are only four cases that can occur in adding the two binary digits (bits) in any position. They are:

0+0=0
1+0=1

1+1=0+carry of 1 into next position
1+1+1=1+carry of 1 into next position

The last case occurs when the two bits in a certain position are 1 and there is a carry from the previous position. Here are several examples of the addition of two binary numbers:

$$
\begin{array}{ccc}
011(3) & 1001(9) & 11.011(3.375) \\
+110(6) & +1111(15) & +10.110(2.750) \\
\hline
1001(9) & 11000(24) & 110.001(6.125)
\end{array}
$$

It is not necessary to consider the addition of more than two binary numbers at a time because in all digital systems the circuitry that actually performs the addition can only handle two numbers at a time. When more than two numbers are to be added, the first two are added together and then their sum is added to the third number, and so on. This is not a serious drawback since modern digital machines can typically perform an addition operation in less than 1 us.

Addition is the most important arithmetic operation in digital systems. As we shall see, the operations of subtraction, multiplication, and division as they are performed in most modern digital computers and calculators actually use only addition as their basic operation.

Summary

Binary system is widely applied in the digital circuit system. The differences between binary and decimal are base and weight. This chapter presents binary numbers, decimal-to-binary conversion and binary arithmetic.

Problems

7.1 Express the decimal number 568.23 as a sum of the values of each digit.

7.2 Convert the binary whole number 1101101 to decimal.

7.3 Convert the fractional binary number 0.1011 to decimal.

7.4 Convert the following decimal numbers to binary:

  (a) 19   (b) 45

7.5 Add the following binary numbers:
  (a) 11+11   (b) 100+10
  (c) 111+11   (d) 110+100

7.6 Perform the following binary subtractions:
  (a) 11−01   (b) 11−10

Chapter 8

Logic Gates

8.1 The Basic Logic Gates

The inverter: A logic circuit that inverts or complements its input.

The AND Gate: A logic gate that produces a HIGH output when all the inputs are HIGH.

The OR Gate: A logic gate that produces a HIGH output when one or more inputs are HIGH.

The NAND Gate: A logic gate that produces a LOW output only when all the inputs are HIGH.

The NOR Gate: A logic gate that produces a LOW output when one or more inputs are HIGH.

Exclusive-OR (XOR) gate: logic gate that produces a HIGH output when its two inputs are at opposite levels.

Exclusive-NOR Gates: A logic gate that produces a LOW when its two inputs are at opposite levels.

Figure 8.1.1 shows the standard logic symbols of these kinds of logic gates.

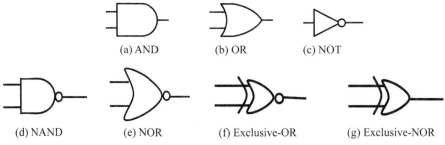

Figure 8.1.1   Standard Logic Symbols

8.2 Fixed-Function Logic

Three kinds of digital logic circuits are CMOS, bipolar, and BiCMOS. They differ in the types of circuit components used internally to implement the logic function. CMOS is implemented with a type of field-effect transistor, bipolar (also known as TTL) logic uses bipolar junction transistors, and BiCMOS employs a combination of both.

All of the basic logic operation, NOT, AND, OR, NAND, NOR, exclusive-OR (XOR), and exclusive-NOR (XNOR) are available in both CMOS and bipolar. IN addition to these, buffered output gates are also available for driving loads that require high currents. The types of gate configurations typically available in IC packages area identified by the last two or three digits in the series designation. For example, 74LS04 is a low-power Schottky hex inverter package. Some of the common logic gate configurations and their standard identifier digits are as follows:

- Quad 2-input NAND—00
- Dual 4-input NAND—20
- Quad 2-input NOR—02
- Quad 2-input AND—21
- Hex inverter—04
- Triple 3-input NOR—27
- Quad 2-input AND—08
- Single 8-input NAND—30
- Triple 3-input NAND—10
- Quad 2-input OR—32
- Triple 3-input AND—11
- Quad XOR—86
- Quad XNOR—266

All of the 74 series CMOS are pin-compatible with the same types of devices in bipolar. This means that a CMOS digital IC such as the 74HC00 (quad 2-input NAND), which contains four 2-input NAND gates in the IC package, has the

Chapter 8 Logic Gates

identical package pin numbers for each input and output as the corresponding bipolar device. Typical IC gate packages, the dual in-line package (DIP) for plug-in or feed through mounting and the small-outline integrated circuit (SOIC) package for surface mounting. In some cases, other types of packages are also available. The SOIC package is significantly smaller than the DIP.

Summary

The basic logic gates and fixed-function logic gates are analyzed in this chapter.

Problems

8.1 The output of an AND gate with inputs A, B and C is a 1(HIGH) when
(a) A=1, B=1, C=1
(b) A=1, B=0, C=1
(c) A=0, B=0, C=0

8.2 The output of an OR gate with inputs A, Band C is a 1(HIGH) when
(a) A=1, B=1, C=1
(b) A=0, B=0, C=1
(c) A=0, B=0, C=0
(d) answers (a), (b), and (c)
(e) only answers (a) and (b)

8.3 The input waveform shown in Figure 3-51is applied to an inverter. Draw the timing diagram of the output waveform in proper relation to the input.

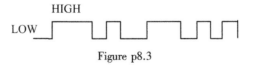

Figure p8.3

8.4 The input waveforms applied to a 4-input AND gate are as indieated in Figure p8.4.Show the output waveform in proper relation to the inputs with a timing diagram.

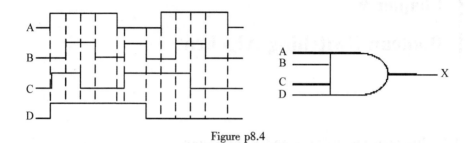

Figure p8.4

8.5 Repeat Problem 8.4 for an exclusive-OR gate.

8.6 Determine the output waveforms for the XOR gate and for the XNOR gate, given the input waveforms, A and B, in Figure p8.6.

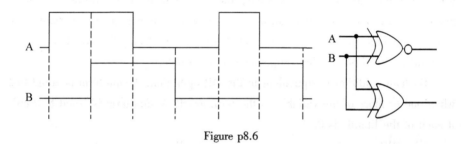

Figure p8.6

Chapter 9

Boolean Switching Algebra

9.1 Boolean Operations and Expressions

Variable, complement are terms used in the Boolean algebra. A variable is a symbol used to represent an action, a condition, or data. Any variable can have only a 1 or 0 value. The complement is the inverse of a variable and is indicated by a bar over the variable. For example, the complement of the variable A is $\overline{A}$. Sometimes a prime rather than an over-bar is used to denote such a variable, for example, B'indicates the complement of B. In this book, only the over-bar is used. A literal is a variable or the complement of a variable.

Boolean Addition is equivalent to the OR operation. A sum term is equal to 1 when one or more of the variable in the term are 1. A sum term is equal to 0 only if each of the literals is 0.

EXAMPLE 1 Determine the values of A, B, C and D that make the sum term $A + \overline{B} + C + \overline{D}$ equal to 0.

SOLUTION For the sum term to be 0, each of the literals in the term must be 0. Therefore, $A = 0, B = 1$ so that $\overline{B} = 0, C = 0$, and $D = 1$ so that $\overline{D} = 0$.

$$A + \overline{B} + C + \overline{D} = 0 + \overline{1} + 0 + \overline{1} = 0 + 0 + 0 + 0 = 0$$

Boolean Multiplication is equivalent to the AND operation. A product term is equal to 1 only if each of the variable is 1. A product term is equal to 0 when one or more of the variables are 0.

EXAMPLE 2 Determine the values of A, B, C and D that make the product term $A\overline{B}C\overline{D}$ equal to 1.

SOLUTION For the product term to be 1, each of the literals in the term must be 1. Therefore, $A = 1$, $\overline{B} = 1$ so that $B = 0$, $C = 1$, and $\overline{D} = 1$ so that $D = 0$.

$$A\bar{B}C\bar{D} = 0 \cdot \bar{1} \cdot 0 \cdot \bar{1} = 1 \cdot 1 \cdot 1 \cdot 1 = 1$$

9.2 Laws and Rules of Boolean Algebra

9.2.1 Laws of Boolean Algebra

Each of the laws is illustrated with two or three variables, but the number of variables is not limited law.

1. Associative

The associative law of multiplication and addition are written as follows for three variables:

$$(xy)z = x(yz)$$
$$(x+y)+z = x+(y+z)$$

This law states that it makes no differences in what order the variables are grouped.

2. Distributive Law

The distributive law is written for three variables as follows:

$$x(y+z) = xy+xz$$

This law states that ORing two or more variable and then ANDing the result with a single variable is equivalent to ANDing the single variable with each of the two or more variables and the ORing the products. Variable x is a factor of both y and z. There is another expression:

$$x+(yz) = (x+y)(x+z)$$

This expression shows the distribution of OR over AND. Variable x can be redistributed over y and z. It is not like an ordinary algebra expression.

3. Commutative Law

The commutative law of addition and multiplication for two variables are:

$$xy = yx$$
$$x+y = y+x$$

This law states that the order in which the variables are ORed or ANDed makes no difference.

9.2.2 Rules of Boolean Algebra

Table 9.2.1 lists 12 basic rules that are useful in manipulating and simplifying Boolean expressions. Rules 1 and 9 will be viewed in terms of their applications to logic gates. Rules 10 through 12 will be derived in terms of the simpler rules and the laws previously discussed.

Table 9.2.1   Basic Rules of Boolean Algebra

1. $A+0=A$	7. $A \cdot A = A$
2. $A+1=1$	8. $A \cdot \bar{A} = 0$
3. $A \cdot 0 = 0$	9. $\bar{\bar{A}} = A$
4. $A \cdot 1 = A$	10. $A+AB=A$
5. $A+A=A$	11. $A+\bar{A}B = A+B$
6. $A+\bar{A}=1$	12. $(A+B)(A+C) = A+BC$

9.3 DeMorgan's Theorems

DeMorgan, an English mathematician, was a contemporary of Boole. He developed a pair of logic theorems that provide a very useful tool for converting logic switching expressions. Both of DeMorgans theorems use the principle of duality.

(1) Demorgan's first theorem is states that the complement of two or more ANDed variable is equivalent to the OR of the complements of the individual variables.

For two variables, expressed mathe matically, this theorem plies that

$$\overline{xy} = \bar{x} + \bar{y}$$

(2) Demorgan's second theorem states that the complement of two or more ORed variable is equivalent to the AND of the complements of the individual variables.

Mathematically, this theorem for two variables implies that

$$\overline{x+y} = \bar{x}\bar{y}$$

In general,

$$\overline{x_1 x_2 x_3 \cdots x_n} = \bar{x}_1 + \bar{x}_2 + \bar{x}_3 + \cdots + \bar{x}_n$$

$$\overline{x_1 + x_2 + x_3 + \cdots + x_n} = \bar{x}_1 \cdot \bar{x}_2 \cdot \bar{x}_3 \cdot \cdots \cdot \bar{x}_n$$

The two theorems can be combined in a single statement. The complement of any switching function can be found by replacing each variable with its complement (x is replaced by $\bar{x}$), each AND with OR, and each OR with AND; constants are replaced by their complements (0 is replaced by 1 and 1 by 0).

9.4 Simplification Using Boolean Algebra

A simplified Boolean expression uses the fewest gates possible to implement a given expression. And they have the same value.

EXAMPLE 3 $\qquad F = x\bar{y}z + xyz$

We want to eliminate the redundant terms.

SOLUTION   By inspection of the two AND terms we find that xz is a factor; therefore, we do the following. By distributive law, $F = xz(y + \bar{y}) = xyz + x\bar{y}z$ also, $y + \bar{y} = 1$ therefore,

$$F = xz$$

They produce the same result in a table, as illustrated by Table 9.4.1.

Table 9.4.1   The Truth Table of Simplification

x	y	z	$x\bar{y}z$	xyz	$x\bar{y}z + xyz$	xz
0	0	0	0	0	0	0
0	0	1	0	0	0	0
0	1	0	0	0	0	0
0	1	1	0	0	0	0
1	0	0	0	0	0	0
1	0	1	1	0	1	1
1	1	0	0	0	0	0
1	1	1	0	1	1	1

In fact, we can use the rules that have been discussed earlier.

EXAMPLE 4 Using Boolean algebra techniques, simplify this expression:
$$AB+A(B+C)+B(B+C)$$
SOLUTION The following is not necessarily the only approach.

Step1: Apply the distributive law to the second and third terms in the expression, as follows:
$$AB+AB+AC+BB+BC$$
step2: Apply rule 7 ($BB=B$) to the fourth term.
$$AB+AB+AC+B+BC$$
step3: Apply rule 5 ($AB+AB=AB$)
$$AB+AC+B+BC$$
step4: Apply rule 10 ($B+BC=B$) to the last two terms.
$$AB+AC+B$$
Step5: Apply rule 10 ($AB+B=B$) to the first and third terms.
$$AC+B$$
At this point the expression is simplified as much as possible.

EXAMPLE 5 Simplify the following Boolean expression:
$$[A\bar{B}(C+BD)+\bar{A}\bar{B}]C$$
SOLUTION Step1: Apply the distributive law to the terms within the brackets.
$$(A\bar{B}C+A\bar{B}BD+\bar{A}\bar{B})C$$
Step2: Apply rule 8 ($B\bar{B}=0$) to the second term within the parentheses, so $A \cdot 0 \cdot D = 0$, Then drop the 0.
$$(A\bar{B}C+\bar{A}\bar{B})C$$
Step3: Apply the distributive law.
$$A\bar{B}CC+\bar{A}\bar{B}C$$
Then apply rule 8 ($CC=C$) to the first term.
$$A\bar{B}C+\bar{A}\bar{B}C$$
Step4: Factor out $\bar{B}C$.
$$\bar{B}C(A+\bar{A})$$
Step5: Apply rule 6($A+\bar{A}+1$). Then drop the 1.
$$\bar{B}C$$

9.5 Boolean Expressions and Truth Tables

9.5.1 The Sum-of-Products (SOP) Form

A product term is the product of literals (variables or their complements). When two or more product terms are summed by Boolean addition, the resulting expression is a sum-of-product (SOP). Some examples are

$$AB+ABC, ABC+CDE+\bar{A}C+D$$

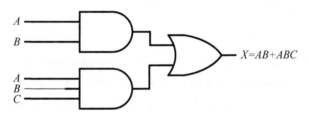

Figure 9.5.1   Implementation of $AB+ABC$

A standard SOP expression is one in which all the variables in the domain of the expression appear in each product term. For example, $ABCD+\bar{A}B\bar{C}D$ is a standard SOP expression. SOP expressions are very important in constructing truth table, and in the Karnaugh map simplification method. Any nonstandard SOP expression can be converted to the standard form using Boolean algebra.

9.5.2 The Product-of-Sums (POS) Form

A sum term is the sum of literals (variables or their complements). When two or more sum terms are multiplied, the resulting expression is a product -of- sum (POS). Some examples are

$$(\bar{A}+B)(A+B+\bar{C})$$
$$(A+B+C)(C+D+E)(\bar{A}+C+D)$$

Figure 9.5.2 shows for the expression $(A+B)(A+B+C)$. The output X of the AND gate equals the POS expression.

A standard POS expression is one in which each sum term contain all the

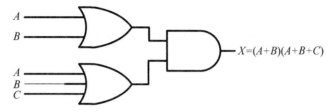

Figure 9.5.2　Implementation of $(A+B)(A+B+C)$

variables in the domain. For example, the expression $(A+C)(B+D)$ has a domain made up of A, B, C, and D. We can see that the sum term don't contain all the variables, so this is not the standard form.

9.5.3　The truth table

A truth table is simply a list of the possible combinations of the input variable values and the corresponding output values (1 or 0). For an expression with a domain of n variables, there are 2^n different combinations of these variables.

This is how to construct a truth table: (1) list all possible combinations of binary values of the variables; (2) put each binary value to the expression, and list the corresponding output value.

EXAMPLE 6　develop a truth table for the $\overline{A}\overline{B}C+A\overline{B}\overline{C}+ABC$

SOLUTION　There are three variables, so there are eight binary values, and list them in the left three columns, see Table 9.5.1.

Table 9.5.1　The Truth Table of EXAMPLE 6

Inputs			Outputs	Production term	
A	B	C	X		
0	0	0	0		
0	0	1	1	$\overline{A}\overline{B}C$	m_1
0	1	0	0		
0	1	1	0		
1	0	0	1	$A\overline{B}\overline{C}$	m_4
1	0	1	0		
1	1	0	0		
1	1	1	1	ABC	m_7

Form the truth table, we get the Boolean expression:

(1) Find the binary values of the input variables which the output is 1;

(2) Convert each value to the product term by replacing each 1 with the corresponding variable and each 0 with the corresponding variable complement. For example, the binary 1010 is converted to a product term as follows:

$$1010 \longrightarrow A\bar{B}C\bar{D}$$

(3) The sum of the product terms are the Boolean expression.

This expression is standard SOP form. We can use m_i to indicate the standard SOP form. The decimal value of the binary value is i. For example,

$$(1010)_{10} \longrightarrow A\bar{B}C\bar{D} \longrightarrow m_{10}$$

so, $\bar{A}\bar{B}C + A\bar{B}\bar{C} + ABC = m_1 + m_4 + m_7 = \sum(m_1, m_4, m_7)$

9.6 The Karnaugh Map

Boolean algebra can be used to simplify equations but the process is lengthy and error-prone. What is needed is a more systematic method for finding and eliminating any redundancies in an equation.

A better approach is the use of the Karnaugh map. Instead of being organized into columns and rows like a truth table, the Karnaugh map is an array of cells in which each cell represents a binary value of the input variables. The cells are arranges in a way so that simplification of a given expression is simply a matter of properly grouping the cells. Karnaugh maps can be used for expression with two, three, four and five variables, but we will just discuss only 3-variable and 4-variable situation to illustrate the principles.

The 3-variable Karnaugh map is an array of eight cells, as show in Figure 9.6.1 (a). In this case, A, B and C are used for the variables. Binary values of A and B are along the left side (notice the sequence) and the values of C are across the top. The value of a given cell is the binary value of A and B at the left in the same row combined with the value of C at the top in the same column. For example, the cell in the lower right corner has a binary value of 101. Figure 9.6.1 (b) shows the standard product terms that are represented by each cell in the Karnaugh map.

Chapter 9 Boolean Switching Algebra

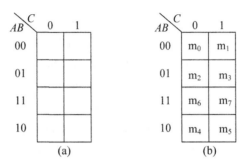

Figure 9.6.1   A 3-variable Karnaugh Map Showing Product Terms

The 4-variable Karnaugh map is an array of sixteen cells, as shown in Figure 9.6.2.

AB\CD	00	01	11	10
00				
01				
11				
10				

AB\CD	00	01	11	10
00	m_0	m_1	m_3	m_2
01	m_4	m_5	m_7	m_6
11	m_{12}	m_{13}	m_{15}	m_{14}
10	m_8	m_9	m_{11}	m_{10}

Figure 9.6.2   A 4-variable Karnaugh Map

Mapping a standard SOP Expression: For a SOP expression in standard form, a 1 is placed on the Karnaugh map for each product term in the expression. Each 1 is placed in a cell corresponding to the value of a product term.

The following steps in Figure 9.6.3 show the mapping process for $\bar{A}+A\bar{B}+AB\bar{C}$

Step1: covert the expression to the standard SOP forms.

$$\bar{A} + A\bar{B} + AB\bar{C} = \sum (m_0, m_1, m_2, m_3, m_4, m_5, m_6)$$

Step2: As each product term, place a 1 on the Karnaugh map, and place 0 for each left.

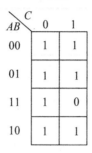

Figure 9.6.3 Mapping a Standard Form

Summary

The most basic digital operations are Boolean Addition and Boolean Multiplication. Logic relationship commonly is represented by expression, truth table or Karnaugh map. We can use Boolean Algebra to simplify Boolean expressions.

Problems

9.1 Apply DeMorgan's theorems to each of the following expressions:

(a) $\overline{(A+B+C)D}$ (b) $\overline{ABC+DEF}$ (c) $\overline{A\bar{B}+\bar{C}D+EF}$

9.2 Apply DeMorgan's theorems to each expression:

(a) $\overline{\overline{(A+B)}+\bar{C}}$ (b) $\overline{(\bar{A}+B)+CD}$ (c) $\overline{(A+B)\overline{CD}+E+\bar{F}}$

9.3 Using Boolean algebra techniques, simplify this expression:

$$AB+A(B+C)+B(B+C)$$

9.4 Simplify the following Boolean expression:

$$[A\bar{B}(C+BD)+\overline{AB}]C$$

Note that brackets and parentheses mean the same thing: the term inside is multiplied (ANDed) with the term outside.

9.5 From the truth table in Table p9.1, determine the standard SOP expression and the equivalent standard POS expression.

Chapter 9 Boolean Switching Algebra

Table p9.1

Inputs			Output
A	B	C	X
0	0	0	0
0	0	1	0
0	1	0	0
0	1	1	1
1	0	0	1
1	0	1	0
1	1	0	1
1	1	1	1

9.6 Map the following standard SOP expression on a Karnaugh map:
$$\bar{A}\bar{B}C+\bar{A}B\bar{C}+AB\bar{C}+ABC$$

9.7 Map the following standard SOP expression on a Karnaugh map:
$$\bar{B}\bar{C}+A\bar{B}+AB\bar{C}+A\bar{B}C\bar{D}+\bar{A}\bar{B}CD+A\bar{B}CD$$

9.8 Determine the product terms for the Karnaugh map in Figure p9.1 and write the resulting minimum SOP expression.

AB \ CD	00	01	11	10
00			1	1
01	1	1	1	1
11	1	1	1	1
10		1		

Figure p9.1

9.9 Use a Karnaugh map to minimize the following SOP expression:
$$\bar{B}\bar{C}\bar{D}+\bar{A}B\bar{C}\cdot\bar{D}+AB\bar{C}\cdot\bar{D}+\bar{A}\cdot\bar{B}CD+A\bar{B}CD+\bar{A}\cdot\bar{B}C\bar{D}+\bar{A}BC\bar{D}+ABC\bar{D}+A\bar{B}C\bar{D}$$

Chapter 10

Combinational Logic

10.1 Definition of Combinational Logic

Combinational logic deals with the techniques of "combining" the basic gates, mentioned previously, into circuits that perform some desired function. Examples of useful combinational logic functions are adders, sub tractors, decoders, encoders, multipliers, dividers, display drivers, and keyboard encoders.

Logic circuits without feedback from output to the input, constructed from a functionally complete gate set, are said to be combinational. Logic circuits that contain no memory (ability to store information) are combinational; those that contain memory, including flip-flops, are said to be sequential. We will study sequential logic in later chapters; for now our task is to develop skills in dealing with combinational logic. Combinational logic can be modeled as illustrated in Figure 10.1.1.

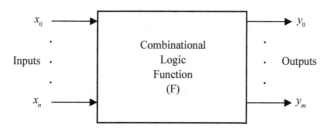

Figure 10.1.1 Combinational Logic Model

Let X be the set of all input variables $\{x_0, x_1, \ldots, x_n\}$, and Y be the set of all output variables $\{y_0, y_1, \ldots, y_m\}$. The combinational function F operates on the input variables set X, to produce the output variable set Y. Notice that the output variables y_0 through y_m are not fed back to the input. The output is related to the input as

$$Y = F(X)$$

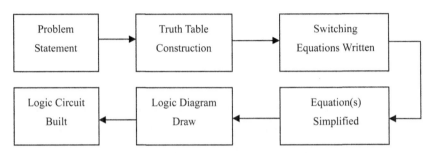

Figure10.1.2 General Logic Design Sequence

The logic circuits developed in chapter 4, illustrating various switching properties and theorems, were all combinational. The relationship between the input and output variables can be expressed in equations, logic diagrams, or truth tables. A truth table specifies the input conditions under which the outputs are true or false (1 or 0). Switching equations are then derived from the truth tables and realized (constructed) using gates.

Before any combinational logic system can be designed it must be defined. Proper statement of a problem is the most important part of any digital design task. Once correctly and clearly stated, any problem can be converted to the necessary logic for implementation. Figure 3.2 illustrates the sequence of design tasks in a general way.

Notice that the first task is to define the problem to be solved. Nothing can occur until that is correctly accomplished. The problem is then "rewritten" in the form of a truth table. From the truth table, the switching equations can be written and simplified and the logic diagram drawn. The logic diagram can be realized using any one of the three main digital integrated circuit families: transistor-transistor logic (TTL), emitter- coupled logic (ECL), or complementary metal-oxide silicon (CMOS). Practical applications rarely come in a prepackaged "truth table," ready for logic design. Truth tables must be constructed from verbal problem descriptions.

10.2 Functions of Combinational Logic

10.2.1 Adders

1. The Half-Adder

The half-adders accept two binary digitals as its inputs and produced two binary digitals as its outputs sum bit and a carry bit.

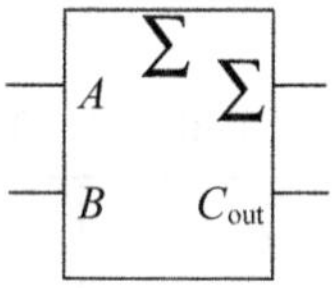

Figure 10.2.1 Logic symbol for a half-adder.

And the truth table shows the operation of it.

Table 10.2.1 Half-adder Truth Table

A	B	C_{out}	Σ
0	0	0	0
0	1	0	1
1	0	0	1
1	1	1	0

From the operation, the expression can be derived for the sum and the output carries as functions of the inputs.

$$\Sigma = A \otimes B$$
$$C_{out} = AB$$

2. The Full-Adder

The full-adder accepts two input bits and an input carry and generates a sum output and an output carry.

The basic difference between a full-adder and half-adder is that if it accepts an input carry.

And the truth table (Table 10.2.2) shows the operation of it.

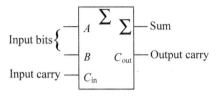

Figure 10.2.2 Logic symbol for a full-adder.

Table 10.2.2 Full-adder Truth Table

A	B	C_{in}	C_{out}	Σ
0	0	0	0	0
0	0	1	0	1
0	1	0	0	1
0	1	1	1	0
1	0	0	0	0
1	0	1	1	0
1	1	0	1	0
1	1	1	1	1

10.2.2 Encoders

Encoders perform a function that is the inverse of decoders. Encoders have multiple inputs and outputs, like decoders. Encoders, however, have more inputs than output variables. The decoder produced 2^n outputs from n inputs. An encoder produces n outputs from 2^n inputs. A typical encoder function can be modeled as shown in Figure 10.2.3.

10.2 Functions of Combinational Logic — 177

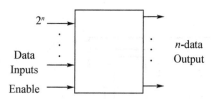

Figure 10.2.3 Typical encoder

1. The Decimal-to-BCD Priority Encoder

This type of encoder performs the same basic encoding function as previously discussed. A priority encoder also offers additional flexibility in that it can be used in applications that require priority detection. The priority means that the encoder will produce a *BCD* output corresponding to the highest-order decimal digit input that is active and will ignore any other lower-order active inputs.

The 74HC147 is a priority encoder with active-LOW inputs (0) for decimal digits 1 through 9 and active-LOW *BCD* outputs as indicated in the logic symbol in Figure 10.2.4.

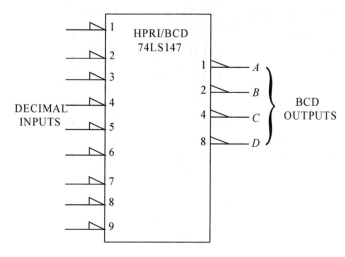

Figure 10.2.4

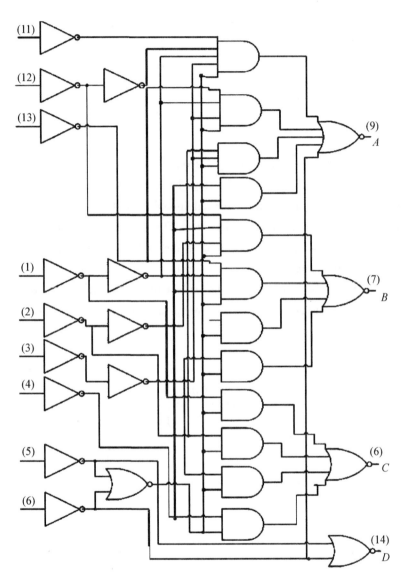

Figure 10.2.4 10-line to BCD Encoder

The function table for the encoder is shown in Table 10.2.3.

Table 10.2.3 Truth Table for a 10-line to BCD Encoder

Decimal value	1	2	3	4	5	6	7	8	9	D	C	B	A
0	1	1	1	1	1	1	1	1	1	1	1	1	1
1	0	1	1	1	1	1	1	1	1	1	1	1	0
2	X	0	1	1	1	1	1	1	1	1	1	0	1
3	X	X	0	1	1	1	1	1	1	1	1	0	0
4	X	X	X	0	1	1	1	1	1	1	0	1	1
5	X	X	X	X	0	1	1	1	1	1	0	1	0
6	X	X	X	X	X	0	1	1	1	1	0	0	1
7	X	X	X	X	X	X	0	1	1	1	0	0	0
8	X	X	X	X	X	X	X	0	1	0	1	1	1
9	X	X	X	X	X	X	X	X	0	0	1	1	0

X indicate a don't-care condition.

2.8-line-to-3-line Priority Encoder

Figure 10.2.5 shows the logic diagram and symbol of another encoder. This priority encoder accepts a three-bit input and produces a 1 out of 23 coded output. It can be expanded by using multiple devices to form even larger value encoding systems. The 1 out of 2' code output structure is used to encode information for transmission to a digital system similar to that described for a 10-line-to-BCD encoder.

Consider a situation where several possible events may occur in an industrial system, and you want to identify an event and assign a code and transmit it to the control unit based on some priority. Such events may be assigned a priority based on their function 1 in the system. By connecting the highest priority event to the highest value input line, the next highest priority event to the next highest input line and so on, down to the lowest priority event being assigned the lowest input line, the device can transmit priority information to the control system. The control system determines a specific course of action to be taken for each event occurrence.

Notice that output GS goes low when any of the inputs to the encoder is active. The purpose of the signal is to communicate to the control system logic that an event has occurred and priority encoded data are present. EO is an active low

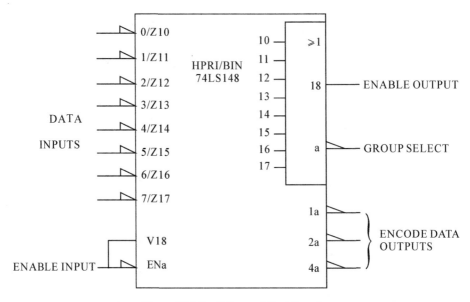

Figure 10.2.5 8-line to 3-line Encoder

signal that can be used to cascade several devices to form a larger priority encoding system. When EO is active no priority event connected to the IC is present. EO is used as the enable input to the next lower priority encoder. The priority encoder truth table is shown in Table 10.2.4.

Table 10.2.4 Truth Table for the 74xx148 8-line to 3-line Priority Encoder

Inputs									Outputs				
EI	0	1	2	3	4	5	6	7	A2	A1	A0	GS	EO
1	X	X	X	X	X	X	X	X	1	1	1	1	1
0	1	1	1	1	1	1	1	1	1	1	1	1	0
0	0	1	1	1	1	1	1	1	1	1	1	0	1
0	X	0	1	1	1	1	1	1	1	1	0	0	1
0	X	X	0	1	1	1	1	1	1	0	1	0	1
0	X	X	X	0	1	1	1	1	1	0	0	0	1
0	X	X	X	X	0	1	1	1	0	1	1	0	1
0	X	X	X	X	X	0	1	1	0	1	0	0	1
0	X	X	X	X	X	X	0	1	0	0	1	0	1
0	X	X	X	X	X	X	X	0	0	0	0	0	1

10.2.3 Multiplexers

A logic symbol for a 4-input multiplexer (MUX) is shown in figure 10.2.6. Notice that there are two data-select lines because with two select bits, any one of the four data-input lines can be selected.

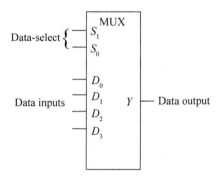

Figure 10.2.6 Logic Symbol for 1-of-4 Data Selector

A summary of this operation is given in table 10.2.5.

Table 10.2.5 Data Selection for a 1-of-4-multiplexer

S_1	S_0	data selscted
0	0	D_0
0	1	D_1
1	0	D_2
1	1	D_3

The data output is equal to D_0 only if $S_1=0$ and $S_0=0$: $Y=D_0\,\overline{S}_1\,\overline{S}_0$
The data output is equal to D_1 only if $S_1=0$ and $S_0=1$: $Y=D_1\,\overline{S}_1\,\overline{S}_0$
The data output is equal to D_2 only if $S_1=1$ and $S_0=0$: $Y=D_2\,S_1\,\overline{S}_0$
The data output is equal to D_3 only if $S_1=1$ and $S_0=1$: $Y=D_3\,S_1\,\overline{S}_0$
When these terms are ORed, the total expression for the data outputs is:
$$Y=D_0\,\overline{S}_1\,\overline{S}_0+D_1\,\overline{S}_1\,\overline{S}_0+D_2\,S_1\,\overline{S}_0+D_3\,S_1\,S_0$$

The 74LS151 has eight data inputs ($D_0 \sim D_7$) and, therefore, three data-select or address input lines ($S_0 \sim S_2$). Three bits are required to select any one of the eight data inputs ($2^3 = 8$). A LOW on the Enable input allows the selected input data to pass through to the output. Notice that the data output and its complement are both available. The pin diagram is shown in Figure 10.2.7.

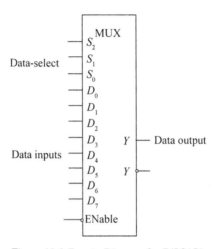

Figure 10.2.7 pin Diagram for 74LS151

The data output is

$$Y = \sum_{i=0}^{7} D_i m_i$$

1. Logic function generators

A useful application of the data selection of the data selector is in the generation logic function in sum-of-products form.

For example, a 74LS151 8-inputs data selector can be used to implement any specified 3-variable logic function if the variable are connected to the data-select inputs and each data input is set to the logic level required in the truth table for the function.

EXAMPLE 1 Implement the logic function specified in table 10.2.6 by using a 74LS151.

Table 10.2.6 the truth table for the function

A	B	C_{in}	Y
0	0	0	0
0	0	1	0
0	1	0	0
0	1	1	1
1	0	0	1
1	0	1	0
1	1	0	1
1	1	1	0

SOLUTION Notice from the truth table that Y is a 1 for the following input variable combinations: 011, 100, and 110. For other combinations, Y is 0. For each of the above-mentioned combinations must be connected to a HIGH (5V). All the other data inputs must be connected to a LOW (ground), as shown in Figure 10.2.8.

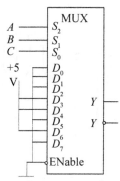

Figure 10.2.8 Data selector connected as function generator

So, the Y is
$$Y = \bar{A}BC + A\bar{B}\bar{C} + AB\bar{C}$$

Summary

Combinational logic deals with the techniques of "combining" the basic

184 — Chapter 10 Combinational Logic

gates, without feedback from output to the input. Adders, decoders and multipliers are discussed in this chapter.

Problems

10.1 For each of the three full-adders in Figure p10.1, determine the outputs for the inputs shown.

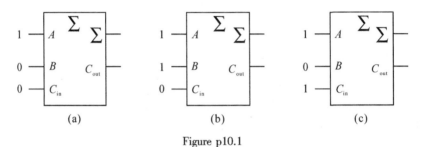

Figure p10.1

10.2 Analyse the function of Figure p10.2 circuit.

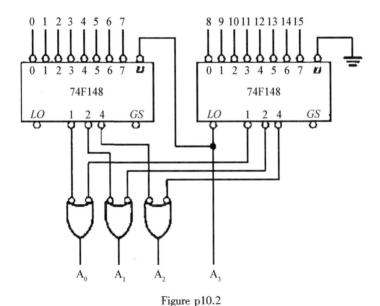

Figure p10.2

10.3 Implement the logic function in Table p10.1 by using a 74LS151 8-input data selector/multiplexer. Compare this method with a discrete logic gate implementation.

Table p10.1

A_3	A_2	A_1	A_0	Y
0	0	0	0	0
0	0	0	1	1
0	0	1	0	1
0	0	1	1	0
0	1	0	0	0
0	1	0	1	1
0	1	1	0	1
0	1	1	1	1
1	0	0	0	1
1	0	0	1	0
1	0	1	0	1
1	0	1	1	0
1	1	0	0	1
1	1	0	1	1
1	1	1	0	0
1	1	1	1	1

10.4 A 74LS151 has alternating LOW and HIGH levels on its data inputs beginning with $D_0 = 0$. The data-select lines are sequenced through a binary count (000, 001, 010, and so on) at a frequency of 1 kHz. The enable input is LOW. Describe the data output waveform.

Chapter 11

Latches, Flip-Flops and Timers

11.1 Latches

11.1.1 The S-R (Set-Reset) Latch

A latch is a type of bitable logic device or multivibrator. An active-LOW input $\overline{S}-\overline{R}$ latch is formed with two cross-coupled NAND gates, as shown in Figure 11.1.1(a). Notice that the output of each gate is connected to an input of the opposite gate. This produces the regenerative feedback that is characteristic of all latches and flip-flops.

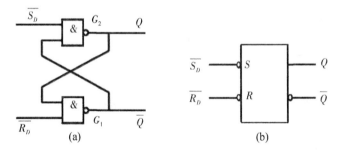

Figure 11.1.1 Basic $\overline{S}-\overline{R}$ Latch

In normal operation, the outputs of a latch are always complements of each other. When Q is HIGH, $\overline{Q}$ is LOW, and when Q is LOW, $\overline{Q}$ is HIGH.

Table 11.1.1 summarizes the logic operation in truth table form.

Table 11.1.1 The Truth Table for Basic $\bar{S}-\bar{R}$ Latch

$\bar{S}$	$\bar{R}$	Q	$\bar{Q}$	
1	1	NC	NC	No change
0	1	1	0	Latch set
1	0	0	1	Latch Reset
0	0	1	1	Invalid condition

The Gated S-R Latch: A gated S-R latch requires an enable input. The logic diagram and logic symbol are shown in Figure 11.1.2.

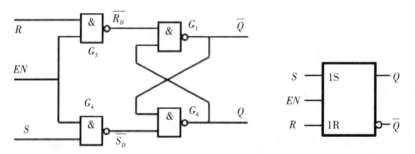

Figure 11.1.2 A Gated Latch

11.2 Flip-Flops

An edge-triggered flip-flop changes state either at the positive edge or the negative edge of the clock pulse and is sensitive to its inputs only at this transition of the clock. Three types of flip-flops are covered in this section: S-R, D, J-K. Although the S-R flip-flop is not available in IC form, it is the basis for the D and J-K flip-flops. The logic symbols for all of these flip-flops are shown in Figure 11.2.1.

11.2.1 The Edge-Triggered S-R Flip-Flop

The S and R inputs of the S-R flip-flop are called synchronous inputs because data on these inputs are transferred to the flip-flop's output only on the triggering

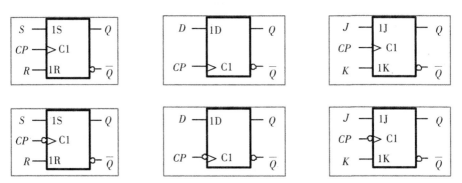

Figure 11.2.1 Edge-triggered Flip-flop Logic Symbols
(Top: positive edge-triggered; Bottom: negative edge-triggered)

edge of the pulse. The basic operation of a position of a positive edge-triggered flip-flop is illustrated in Table 11.2.1.

Table 11.2.1 Truth Table for Positive Edge-triggered S-R flip-flop

S	R	CLK	Q	$\overline{Q}$	Comment
0	0	X	Q_0	$\overline{Q}_0$	No change
0	1	↑	0	1	Latch Reset
1	0	↑	1	0	Latch set
1	1	↑	?	?	Invalid condition

11.2.2 The Edge-Triggered D Flip-Flop

The D flip-flop is useful when a single data bit (1 or 0) is to be stored. The addition of an inverter to an S-R flip-flop creates a basic D flip-flop, as in Figure 11.2.2, where a positive edge-triggered type is shown.

11.2.3 The Edge-Triggered J-K Flip-Flop

The J-K flip-flop is versatile and is a widely used type of flip-flop. The difference is that the J-K flip-flop has no invalid state as does the S-R flip-flop. Table 11.2.2 summarizes the logical operation of the J-K flip-flop.

11.2 Flip-Flops

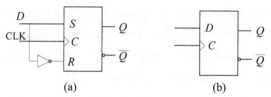

Figure 11.2.2   A Positive Edge-triggered D Flip-flop

Table 11.2.2   the Truth Table for Positive Edge-triggered J-K Flip-flop

J	K	CLK	Q	$\bar{Q}$	Comment
0	0	↑	Q_0	$\bar{Q}_0$	No change
0	1	↑	0	1	Latch Reset
1	0	↑	1	0	Latch set
1	1	↑	$\bar{Q}_0$	Q_0	Toggle

11.2.4 Flip-Flop Applications

1. Parallel data storage

A common requirement in digital systems is to store several bits of data from parallel lines simultaneously in a group of flip-flop. This operation is illustrated in Figure 11.2.3 using four D flip-flops. Each of the four parallel data lines is connected to the D input of a flip-flop. The clock inputs are connected together, so that each flip-flop is triggered by the same clock pulse. This group of four flip-flops is an example of a basic register used for data storage.

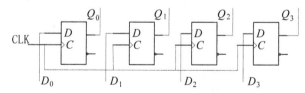

Figure 11.2.3   Flip-flops Used in a Basic Register for Parallel Data Storage

2. Frequency division

Another application of a flip-flop is to divide the frequency of a periodic waveform. When a pulse waveform is applied to the clock input of a J-K flip-flop that is connected to toggle ($J=K=1$), the Q output is a square wave with one-half the frequency of the clock input. Thus, a single flip-flop can be applied as a divide-by-2 device, as in illustrated in Figure 11.2.4.

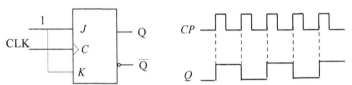

Figure 11.2.4 J-K Flip-flop as a Divide-by-2 Device and the Waveform

3. Counting

Another important application of flip-flops is in digital counters. The flip-flops are negative edge-triggered J-Ks. Both flip-flops are initially RESET (Q LOW). Figure 11.2.5 illustrates the changes in the state of the flip-flop outputs in response to the clock pulses. Both flip-flops are connected for toggle operation ($J=K=1$).

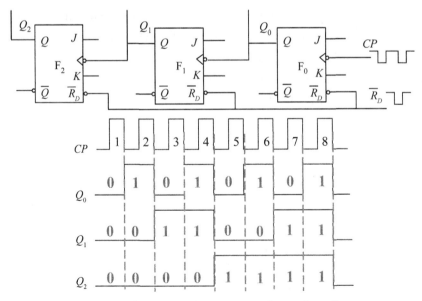

Figure 11.2.5 Flip-flops Used to Generate a Binary Count Sequence

11.3 One-shots

If a device has two states: unstable and stable state, we can called the device a one shot. The output of inverter goes HIGH (unstable state) in response to the trigger input. It mains HIGH for a time set by the RC time constant. At the end of the time, it goes LOW (stable state).

A nonretriggerable one-shot will not respond to any additional trigger pulses from the time it is triggered into its unstable state until it returns to its stable state. In other words, it will ignore any trigger pulses occurring before it times out. The time that the one-shot remains in its unstable state are the pulse width of the output, we can call it t_w.

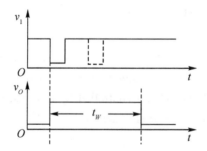

Figure 11.3.1 The Nonretriggerable One-shot

The 555 timer is a versatile and widely used IC device because it can be configured in two different modes as either a monostable multivibrator (one-shot) or as a stable multivibrator (pulse oscillator).

The 555 timer operation: A functional diagram showing the internal components of a 555 timer is shown in Figure 11.3.2.

The comparators are devices whose outputs are HIGH when the voltage across the positive (+) input greater than the voltage across the negative (−) input and LOW when the−input voltage is greater than the+input voltage. The voltage divider consisting of three 5kΩ resistors provides a trigger level of 1/3 Vcc and a threshold of 2/3 V_{CC}. The control voltage input (pin 5) can be used to externally adjust the

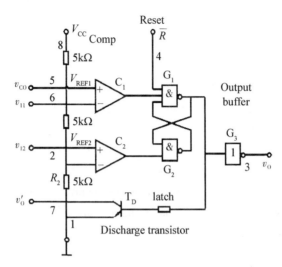

Figure 11.3.2 Internal Functional of 555 Timers

trigger and threshold levels to other values if necessary. The external reset input can be used to reset the latch independent of the threshold circuit. The trigger and threshold inputs (pins 2 and 6) are controlled by external components connected to produce either monostable or astable action.

Table 11.3.1 555 Timer Operation

Input			Output	
V_{11}	V_{12}	R_D	V_O	T_D
×	×	0	0	Turn on
$<\frac{2}{3}V_{CC}$	$<\frac{1}{3}V_{CC}$	1	1	Turn off
$>\frac{2}{3}V_{CC}$	$>\frac{1}{3}V_{CC}$	1	0	Turn on
$<\frac{2}{3}V_{CC}$	$>\frac{1}{3}V_{CC}$	1	No change	No change

11.3 One-shots

An external resistor and capacitor as shown in Figure 11.3.3 are used to set up the 555 timer as a nonretriggerable one-shot. The pulse width of the output is determined by the time constant of R1 and C1 according to the following formula

$$t_w = 1.1 R_1 C_1$$

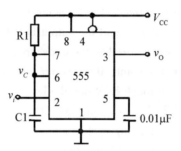

Figure 11.3.3 555 Timer Connected as a One-shot

Before a trigger pulse is applied, the output is LOW and the discharge transistor T is on, keeping C1 discharged as shown in Figure 11.3.4(b). When a negative-going trigger pulse is applied, the output goes HIGH and the discharge transistor turns off, allowing capacitor C1 to begin charging through R1, as shown in Figure 11.3.4(a).

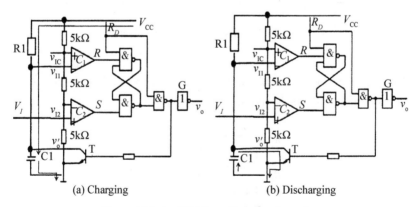

Figure 11.3.4 555 Timer One-shot Operation

11.4 The Astable Multivibrator

Figure 11.4.1 (a) shows a simple form of astable multivibrator with Schimitt trigger and an RC circuit connected in a feedback arrangement.

When the power is first applied, the capacitor has no charge; so the input to the Schmitt trigger inverter is LOW and the output is HIGH. The capacitor charges through R until the input voltage reaches the upper trigger point (VT+), as shown in Figure 11.4.1 (b). At this point, the inverter output goes LOW, causing the capacitor to discharge back through R. When the inverter input voltage decreases to the lower trigger point (VT−), its output goes HIGH and the capacitor charges again. This charging and discharging cycle continues to repeat as long as power is applied to the circuit, and the resulting output is a pulse waveform, as indicated.

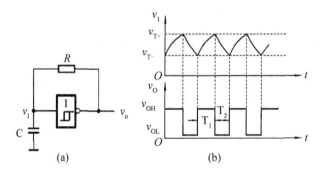

Figure 11.4.1 Basic Astable Multivibrator

The 555 Timer as an mulitivibrator: A 555 timer connected to operate as an astable mulitivibrator is shown in Figure 11.4.2.

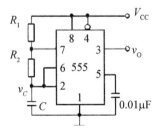

Figure 11.4.2 555 Timer Connected as an Astable Multivibrator

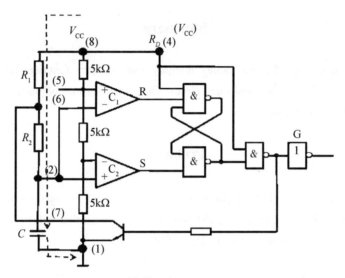

(a) Charging

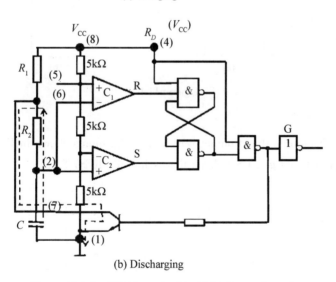

(b) Discharging

Figure 11.4.3   555 Timer Astable Multivibrator Operation

We can calculate the time of HIGH and LOW of the output.
$$T_1 = 0.7(R_1 + R_2)C$$
$$T_2 = 0.7R_2C_1$$

Summary

Latch and Flip-Flop are binary memory with memory function. They are the basic devices of the sequential logic circuit. The 555 timer can be used as One-shot and actable multivibrator.

Problems

11.1 If the $\overline{S}$ and $\overline{R}$ waveforms in Figure p11.1(a) are applied to the inputs of the latch in Figure p11.1(b), determine the waveform that will be observed on the Q output. Assume that Q is initially LOW.

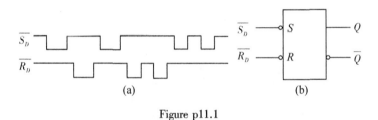

Figure p11.1

11.2 Determine the Q output waveform if the inputs shown in Figure p11.2 (a) are applied to a gated S-R latch that is initially RESET.

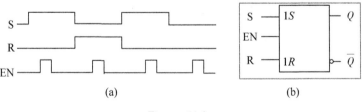

Figure p11.2

11.3 Given the waveforms in Figure p11.3(a) for the D input and the clock, determine the Q output waveform if the flip-flop starts out RESET.

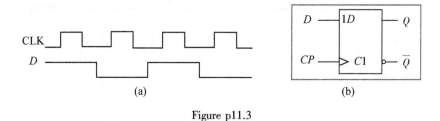

Figure p11.3

11.4 The waveforms in Figure p11.4(a) are applied to the J, K and clock inputs as indicated. Determine the Q output, assuming that the flip-flop is initially RESET.

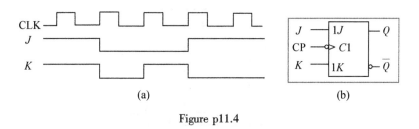

Figure p11.4

11.5 The waveforms in Figure p11.5(a) are applied to the flip-flop as shown. Determine the Q output, starting in the RESET state.

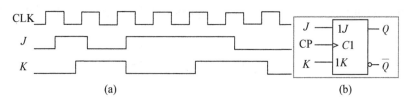

Figure p11.5

11.6 Determine the output waveforms in relation to the clock for Q_A, Q_B, and Q_C in the circuit of Figure p11.6 and show the binary sequence represented by these waveforms.

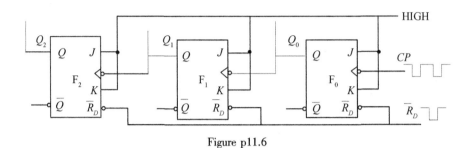

Figure p11.6

11.7 What is the output pulse width for a 555 monostable circuit with $R_1 = 2.2\text{k}\Omega$ and $C_1 = 0.01\,\mu\text{F}$?

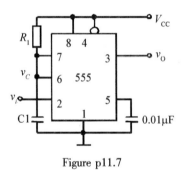

Figure p11.7

11.8 A 555 timer configured to run in the astable mode (pulse oscillator) is shown in Figure p11.8. Determine the frequency of the output and the duty cycle.

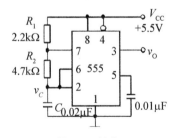

Figure p11.8

Chapter 12

Counters and Shift Registers

12.1 Counters

12.1.1 Asynchronous Counters

According to the Figure 12.1.1 in 11-2, flip-flops used to generate a binary count sequence. It is a sample of asynchronous counters. Because the three flip-flops are never simultaneously triggered, so the counter operation is asynchronous.

Table 12.1.1 State Sequence for a 3-bit Binary Counter

Clock pulse	Q_2	Q_1	Q_0
initially	0	0	0
1	0	0	1
2	0	1	0
3	0	1	1
4	1	0	0
5	1	0	1
6	1	1	0
7	1	1	1
8	0	0	0

The 74LS293 is an example of a specific integrated circuit asynchronous counter. As the logic diagram in Figure 12.1.1, this device actually consists of a single flip-flop and a 3-bit asynchronous counter. This arrangement is for flexibility.

It can be used as a divide-by-2 device if only the single flip-flop is used, or it can be used as a modulus-8 counter if only the 3-bit counter portion is used. This device also provides gated reset inputs, RO (1) and RO (2). When both of these inputs are HIGH, the counter is reset to the 0000 state.

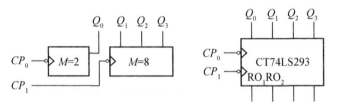

Figure 12.1.1   74LS293

Additionally, the 74LS293 can be used as a 4-bit modulus-16 counter (counts 0 through 15) by connecting the Q0 output to the CP1 input as shown in Figure 12.1.2.

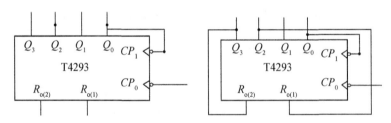

(a) 74LS293 Connected as a Modulus-16 Counter   (b) 74LS293 Connected as a Modulus-12 Counter

Figure 12.1.2

12.1.2 Synchronous Counters

If all the flip-flops are simultaneously triggered, the counter operation is synchronous. The 74LS161 is an example of an integrated circuit 4-bit synchronous binary counter. A logic symbol is shown in Figure 12.1.3 with ping numbers in parentheses.

12.1 Counters 201

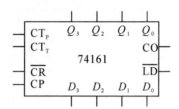

Figure 12.1.3 74LS161

Table 12.1.2 74LS161 Operation

Input									Output			
$\overline{CR}$	$\overline{LD}$	CP_T	CT_P	CP	D_0	D_1	D_2	D_3	Q_0	Q_1	Q_2	Q_3
0	×	×	×	×	×	×	×	×	0	0	0	0
1	0	×	×	↑	d_0	d_1	d_2	d_3	d_0	d_1	d_2	d_3
1	1	1	1	↑	×	×	×	×	count			
1	1	0	×	×	×	×	×	×	No change, $CO=0$			
1	1	1	0	×	×	×	×	×	No change			

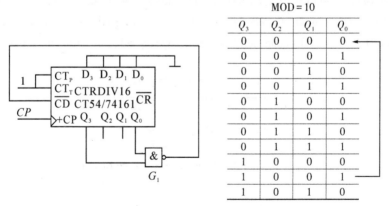

(a) 74LS161 modulus-10 counter using $\overline{LD}$

Figure 12.1.4 74LS161 Connected as a Modulus-10 Counter(1)

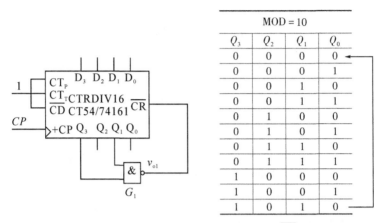

(b) 74LS161 modulus-10 counter using $\overline{CR}$

Figure 12.1.4 74LS161 Connected as a Modulus-10 Counter(2)

12.2 Shift Registers

A register is a digital circuit with two basic functions: data storage and data movement. The storage capability of a register makes it an important type of memory device. Figure 12.2.1 illustrates the concept of storing a 1 or 0 in a D flip-flop. When a 1 is on D, Q becomes a 1 at the triggering edge of CLK and remains. When a 0 is on D, Q becomes a 0 at the triggering edge of CLK and remains.

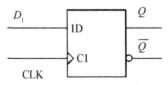

Figure 12.2.1 The Flip-flop as a Storage Element

The storage capacity of a register is the total number of bits (1s and 0s) of digital data it can retain. Each stage in a shift register represents one bit of storage capacity. The shift capability of a register permits the movement of data from stage

12.2 Shift Registers

to stage within the register or into or out of the register upon application of clock pulses.

Let's first look at the serial entry of data into a typical shift register. Figure 12.2.2 shows a 4-bit device implemented with D flip-flops.

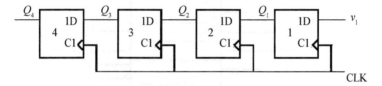

Figure 12.2.2 4-bit Serial in/serial Out Shift Register

Figure 12.2.3 illustrates entry of the four bits 1011 into the register, beginning with the most significant bit. The register is initially clear.

If you want to get the data out of the register, the bits must be shifted out serially and taken off the Q_3 output. After 8 CLKs, all zeros are shown being shifted in.

CLK	Input data	Data in shift register			
		Q_0	Q_1	Q_2	Q_3
0		0	0	0	0
1	1	1	0	0	0
2	0	0	1	0	0
3	1	1	0	1	0
4	1	1	1	0	1
5	0	0	1	1	0	1 from Q_3
6	0	0	0	1	1	0 from Q_3
7	0	0	0	0	1	1 from Q_3
8	0	0	0	0	0	1 from Q_3

Figure 12.2.3 Four Bits (1011) Being Entered Serially into the Register

The 74HC195 is an example of an IC Shift register that can be used for parallel in/parallel out operation. The operation can be seen in Figure 12.2.4.

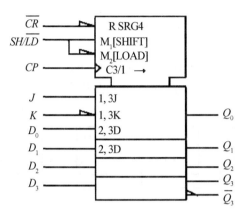

$\overline{CR}$	$SH/\overline{LD}$	CP	J	$\bar{K}$	D_0	D_1	D_2	D_3	Q_0	Q_1	Q_2	Q_3	$\overline{Q}_3$
0	×	×	×	×	×	×	×	×	0	0	0	0	1
1	0	↑	×	×	d_0	d_1	d_2	d_3	d_0	d_1	d_2	d_3	$\bar{d}_3$
1	1	↑	0	1	×	×	×	×	Q_0^n	Q_0^n	Q_1^n	Q_2^n	$\overline{Q}_2^n$
1	1	↑	0	0	×	×	×	×	0	Q_0^n	Q_0^n	Q_1^n	$\overline{Q}_1^n$
1	1	↑	1	0	×	×	×	×	$\overline{Q}_0^n$	0	Q_0^n	Q_0^n	$\overline{Q}_0^n$
1	1	↑	1	1	×	×	×	×	1	1	0	Q_0^n	$\overline{Q}_0^n$
1	1	0	×	×	×	×	×	×	Q_0^n	Q_1^n	Q_2^n	Q_3^n	$\overline{Q}_3^n$

Figure 12.2.4　74HC195 Operation

Summary

This chapter introduces the way to design scheduling logic circuit with medium-scale integrated counter and shift register.

Problems

12.1　Choice question:

(1) Asynchronous counters are known as (　　).

(a) ripple counters (b) multiple clock counters
(c) decade counters (d) modulus counters

(2) An asynchronous counter differs from a asynchronous counter in (　).
   (a) the number of states in its sequence
   (b) the method of clocking
   (c) the type of flip-flops used
   (d) the value of the modulus

(3) The modulus of a counter is (　).
   (a) the number of flip-flops
   (b) the actual number of states in its sequence
   (c) the number of times it recycles in a second
   (d) the maximum possible number of states

(4) A 3-bit binary counter has a maximum modulus of (　).
   (a) 3   (b) 6
   (c) 8   (d) 16

(5) A modulus-12 counter must have (　).
   (a) 12 flip-flops   (b) 3 flip-flops
   (c) 4 flip-flops   (d) synchronous clocking

(6) Three cascaded modulus-10 counters have an overall modulus of (　).
   (a) 30   (b) 100
   (c) 1000   (d) 10,000

(7) A 10MHz clock frequency is applied to a cascaded counter consisting of a modulus-5 counter, a modulus-8 counter, and two modulus-10 counters. The lowest output frequency possible is (　).
   (a) 10kHz   (b) 2.5kHz
   (c) 5 kHz   (d) 25 kHz

(8) The terminal count of a modulus-13 binary counter is (　).
   (a) 0000   (b) 1111
   (c) 1101   (d) 1100

(9) A stage in a shift register consists of (　).
   (a) a latch   (b) a flip-flop
   (c) a byte of storage (d) four bits of storage

(10) To serially shift a byte of data into a shift register, there must be (　).

(a) one clock pulse (b) one load pulse
(c) eight clock pulse (d) one clock pulse for each 1 in the data

(11) To parallel load a byte of data into a shift register with a synchronous load, there must be (　　).

(a) one clock pulse (b) one clock pulse for each 1 in the data
(c) eight clock pulse (d) one clock pulse for each 0 in the data

(12) The group of bits 10110101 is serially shifted (right-most bit first) into an 8-bit parallel output shift register with an initial state of 11100100. After two clock pulses, the register contains (　　).

(a) 01011110 (b) 10110101
(c) 01111001 (d) 00101101

12.2 If the output is connected back to the serial input, a shift register can be used as a ring counter. Determine Figure p12.1 its application with a 74HC195 4-bit shift register.

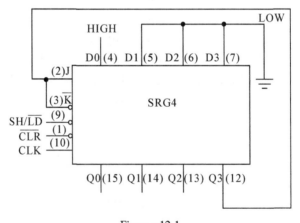

Figure p12.1

12.3 Use 74HC195 4-bit shift registers to implement a 16-bit ring counter. Show the connections.

Appendix A

Testing Solid-state Components

Procedure 1: Testing A Diode

Step 1. Connect the ohmmeter leads to the diode. Notice if the meter indicates continuity through the diode or not.

Step 2. Reverse the diode connection to the ohmmeter. Notice if the meter indicates continuity through the diode or not. The ohmmeter should indicate continuity through the diode in only one direction. (Note: If continuity is not indicated in either direction, the diode is open. If continuity is indicated in both directions, the diode is shorted.)

Procedure 2: Testing A Transistor

Step 1. Using a diode, determine which ohmmeter lead is positive and which is negative. The ohmmeter will indicate continuity through the diode only when the positive lead is connected to the anode of the diode and the negative lead is connected to the cathode.

Step 2. If the transistor is an NPN, connect the positive ohmmeter lead to the base and the negative lead to the collector. The ohmmeter should indicate continuity. The reading should be about the same as the reading obtained when the diode was tested.

Step 3. with the positive ohmmeter lead still connected to the base of the transistor, connect the negative lead to the emitter. The ohmmeter should again indicate a forward diode junction. (Note: If the ohmmeter does not indicate continuity between the base-collector or the base-emitter, the transistor is open.)

Step 4. Connect the negative ohmmeter lead to the base and the positive lead to the collector. The ohmmeter should indicate infinnity or no continuity.)

Step 5. With the negative ohmmeter lead connected to the base, reconnect the positive lead to the emitter. There should again be no indication of continuity. (Note: If a very high resistance is indicated by the ohmmeter, the transistor is "leaky" but may still operate in the circuit. If a very low resistance is seen, the transistor is shorted.)

Step 6. To test a PnP transistor, reverse the polarity of the ohmmeter leads and repeat the test. When the negative ohmmeter lead is connected to the base, a forwatd diode junction should be indicated when the positive lead is connected to the collector or emitter.

Step 7. If the positive ohmmeter lead is connected to the base of a PNP transistor, no continuity should be indicated when the negative lead is connected to the collector or the emitter.

Procedure 3: Testing A Unijunction Transistor

Step 1. Using a junction mode, determine which ohmmeter lead is positive and which is negative. The ohmmeter will indicate continuity when the positive lead is connected to the anode and the negative lead is connected to the cathode.

Step 2. Connect the postive ohmmeter lead to the emitter lead an the negative lead to the base #1. The ohmmeter should indicate a forward diode junction.

Step 3. With the postive ohmmeter lead connected to the emitter, reconnect the negative lead to base #2. The ohmmeter should again indicate a forward diode junction.

Step 4. If the negative ohmmeter lead is connected to the emitter, no continuitu should be indicated when the positive lead is connected to either base #1 or base #2.

Procedure 4: Testing An SCR

Step 1. Using a junction diode, determine which ohmmeter lead is positive and which is negative. The ohmmeter will indicate continuity only when the positive lead is connected to the anode of the diode and negative lead is connected to the cathode.

Step 2. Connect the positive ohmmeter lead to the anode of the SCR and the negative lead to the cathode. The ohmmeter should indicate no continuity.

Step 3. Using a jumper lead, connect the gate of the SCR to the anode. The ohmmeter should indicate a forward diode junction whien the connection is made. (Note: If the jumper is removed, the SCR may continue to conduct or it may turn off. This will be determined by whether the ohmmeter can supply enough current to keep SCR above its holding-current level or not.)

Step 4. Reconnect the SCR so that the cathode is connected to the postive ohmmeter lead and the anode is connected to the negative lead. The ohmmeter should indicate no continuity.

Step 5. If a jumper lead is used to connect the gate to the anode, the ohmmeter should indicate no continuity. (Note: SCRs designed to switch large currents (50 amperes or more) may indicate some leakage current with this test. This is normal fo some devices.)

Procedure 5: Testing A Triac

Step 1. Using a junction diode, determine which ohmmeter lead is positive and which is negative. The ohmmeter will indicate continuity only when the positive lead is connected to the anode an the negative lead is connected to the cathode.

Step 2. Connect the positive ohmmeter lead to MT2 and the negative lead to MT1. The ohmmeter should indicate no continuity through the triac.

Step 3. Using a jumper lead, connect the gate of the triac to MT2. The ohmmeter should indicate a forward diode junction.

Step 4. Reconnect the triac so that MT1 is connected to the positive ohmmeter lead and MT2 is connected to the negative lead. The ohmmeter should indicate no continuity through the triac.

Step 5. Using a jumper leadm, again connect the gate to MT2. The ohmmeter should indicate a forward should diode junction.

Appendix B

Answers to All the Problems

Chapter 1

1.1 An "ideal" device or system is one that has the characteristics we would prefer to have when using a device or system in a practical application. Usually, however, technology only permits a close replica of the desired characteristics. The "ideal" characteristics provide an excellent basis for comparison with the actual device characteristics permitting an estimate of how well the device or system will perform. On occasion, the "ideal" device or system can be assumed to obtain a good estimate of the overall response of the design. When assuming an "ideal" device or system there is no regard for component or manufacturing tolerances or any variation from device to device of a particular lot.

1.2 In the forward-bias region the 0V drop across the diode at any level of current results in a resistance level of zero ohms – the "on" state – conduction is established. In the reverse-bias region the zero current level at any reverse-bias voltage assures a very high resistance level – the open-circuit of "off" state – conduction is interrupted.

1.3 The most important difference between the characteristics of a diode and a simple switch is that the switch, being mechanical, is capable of conducting current in either direction while the diode only allows charge to flow through the element in one direction (specifically the direction defined by the arrow of the symbol using conventional current flow).

1.4 (a) $I_D = I_R = \dfrac{E - V_D}{R} = \dfrac{30\text{V} - 0.7\text{V}}{2.2\text{k}\Omega} = 13.32\text{mA}$

$V_D = 0.7\text{V}, V_R = E - V_D = 30\text{V} - 0.7\text{V} = 29.3\text{V}$

(b) $I_D = I_R = \dfrac{E - V_D}{R} = \dfrac{30\text{V} - 0\text{V}}{2.2\text{k}\Omega} = 13.64\text{mA}$

$V_D = 0V, V_R = 30V$

(c) yes, when $E \gg V_T$, the levels of I_D and V_R are quite close.

1.5 (a) Diode forward-biased, Kirchhoff's voltage law (cw): $-5V + 0.7V - V_O = 0V \Rightarrow V_O = -4.3V$

$$I_R = I_D = \frac{|V_O|}{R} = \frac{4.3V}{2.2k\Omega} = 1.955mA$$

(b) Diode forward-biased,

$$I_D = \frac{8V - 0.7V}{1.2k\Omega + 4.7k\Omega} = 1.24mA$$

$$V_O = V_{4.7k\Omega} + V_D = (1.24mA)(4.7k\Omega) + 0.7V = 6.53V$$

1.6 $V_{dc} = 0.318 V_m \Rightarrow V_m = \frac{V_{dc}}{0.318} = \frac{2V}{0.318} = 6.28V$

$$I_m = \frac{V_m}{R} = \frac{6.28V}{2.2k\Omega} = 2.85mA$$

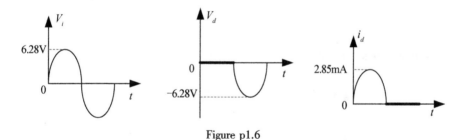

Figure p1.6

1.7 $V_{dc} = 0.318 V_m \Rightarrow V_m = \frac{V_{dc}}{0.318} = \frac{2V}{0.318} = 6.28V$

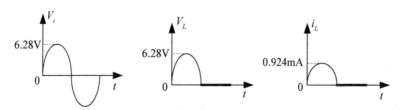

Figure p1.7

$$I_{Lmax} = \frac{v_L}{R_L} = \frac{6.28\text{V}}{6.8\text{k}\Omega} = 0.924\text{mA}$$

1.8 (a) $V_m = \sqrt{2}(120\text{V}) = 169.7\text{V}$

$V_{LM} = V_{im} - 2V_p = 169.7\text{V} - 1.4\text{V} = 168.3\text{V}$

$V_{dc} = 0.363(168.3\text{V}) = 107.04\text{V}$

(b) $\text{PIV} = V_{m(\text{load})} + V_D = 168.3\text{V} + 0.7\text{V} = 169\text{V}$

(c) $I_{D(\text{MAX})} = \frac{V_{LM}}{R_L} = \frac{168.3\text{V}}{1\text{k}\Omega} = 168.3\text{mA}$

(d) $P_{(\text{MAX})} = V_D I_D = (0.7\text{V}) I_{\text{MAX}} = (0.7\text{V})(168.3\text{mA}) = 117.81\text{mW}$

1.9 (a) Positive pulse of v_i:

$v_o = (v_i - 0.7\text{V}) \frac{1.2\text{k}\Omega}{2.2\text{k}\Omega + 1.2\text{k}\Omega} = (10\text{V} - 0.7\text{V}) \frac{1.2\text{k}\Omega}{3.4\text{k}\Omega} = 3.28\text{V}$

Negative pulse v_i:

Diode "open", $v_o = 0\text{V}$

(b) Positive pulse of v_i:

$v_o = v_i - 0.7\text{V} + 5\text{V} = 10\text{V} + 4.3\text{V} = 14.3\text{V}$

Negative pulse v_i:

Diode "open", $v_o = 0\text{V}$

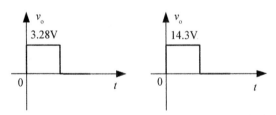

Figure p1.9

1.10 For the positive region of v_i:

The right s_i diode is reverse-biaoed.

The left s_i diode is "on" for levels of v_i greater than $5.3\text{V} + 0.7\text{V} = 6\text{V}$. In fact, $v_o = 6\text{V}$ for $v_i \geq 6\text{V}$.

For $v_i < 6\text{V}$ both diodes are reverse-biaoed and $v_o = v_i$.

For the negative region of v_i:

The left s_i diode is reverse-biaoed.

The right s_i diode is "on" for levels of v_i more negative than $7.3V+0.7V=8V$. In fact, $v_o=-8V$ for $v_i \leqslant -8V$.

For $v_i > -8V$ both diodes are reverse-biaoed and $v_o = v_i$.

i_R: For $-8V < v_i < 6V$ there is no conduction through the 10kΩ resistor due to the lack of a complete circuit. Therefore, $i_R = 0mA$.

For $v_i \geqslant 6V$, $v_R = v_i - v_o = v_i - 6V$

For $v_i = 10V$, $v_R = 10V - 6V = 4V$ and $i_R = \dfrac{4V}{10k\Omega} = 0.4mA$

For $v_i \leqslant -8V$, $v_R = v_i - v_o = v_i + 8V$
For $v_i = -10V$, $v_i = -10V$, $v_R = -10V + 8V = -2V$

and $i_R = \dfrac{-2V}{10k\Omega} = -0.2mA$

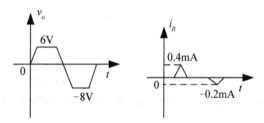

Figure p1.10

Chapter 2

2.1 A bipolar transistor utiliges holes and electrons in the injection or change flow process, while unipolar devices? either electrons or holes, but not both, in the change flow process.

2.2 $I_B = \dfrac{1}{100} I_C \rightarrow I_C = 100 I_B$

$I_E = I_C + I_B = 100 I_B + I_B = 101 I_B$

$I_B = \dfrac{I_E}{101} = \dfrac{8mA}{101} = 79.21 \mu A$

$I_C = 100 I_B = 100(79.21 \mu A) = 7.921 mA$

2.3

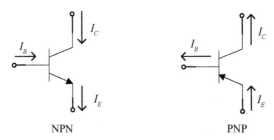

Figure p2.3

2.4 Current relationship of the three electrodes: $(1) I_E = I_B + I_C$ (2) An NPN transistor, the direction of emitter current is outflow, the direction of current collector and base is inflow. A PNP transistor, the direction of emitter current is inflow, collector and base are outflow direction.

(a) The current direction of the two transistors is inflow shown in the Fig, the base current is 0.1mA, the collector current is 0.4mA, the current of the remaining electrode emitter $I_E = I_B + I_C = 4.1\text{mA}$, the current direction is outflow, the type is determined based on the current direction NPN type. As is shown in Figure p2.4(a).

(b) One of the current direction is inflow shown in the Fig, the other is outflow. So the emitter current is 6.1mA, and the remaining current is 6.1mA − 0.1mA = 6mA, the current direction is outflow, and because 0.1mA < 6mA, it is the collector current of 6mA, the type is PNP. As is shown in Figure p2.4(b).

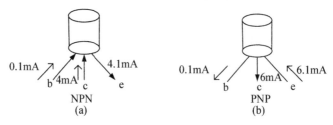

Figure p2.4

2.5 The external conditions that transistor working in the amplifying region need to meet are: emitter junction is forward biased, collector reverse bias. For the NPN-type, the potential between the three pole is: $V_E < V_B < V_C$; For the PNP type, the potential between the three pole is: $V_E > V_B > V_C$; Therefore in amplifier circuit, the base potential is the intermediate potential regardless of the type, so we can determine the base at first. Additionally, the positive bias voltage of emitter is typical, if silicon type, positive bias voltage of 0.7V, if germanium type, positive bias voltage of 0.2V, so that can determine the emitter and collector electrodes. Finally, according to the size of the potential of the three poles, can determine the type of the transistors.

Because $V_A < V_C < V_B$, the electrode C is the base b, $V_B - V_C = 0.2V$, whereby to determine the electrode B is the emitter e, the remaining electrode A is the collector c. Therefore $V_E < V_B < V_C$, this is NPN type.

2.6 If the emitter junction is forward biased, collector junction reverse bias, the transistor work in the amplifying region; If the emitter and collector junction is forward biased, the transistor work in the saturation region; If the emitter and collector junction reverse bias, the transistor work in the cutoff region.

(a) $V_{BE} = 2.7V - 2V = 0.7V > 0$, Emitter junction is forward biased, $V_{BC} = 2.7V - 5V = -2.3V < 0$, Collector junction reverse biased, so the transistor work in the active region.

(b) $V_{BE} = 1.5V - 2V = -0.5V < 0$, Emitter junction reverse bias, $V_{BC} = 1.5V - 7V = -5.5V < 0$, Collector junction reverse bias, so the transistor work in the cutoff region.

(c) $V_{EB} = 5.7V - 5V = 0.7V > 0$, Emitter junction is forward biased, $V_{CB} = 7V - 5V = 2V > 0$, Collector junction is forward biased, so the transistor work in the saturation region.

2.7 a. $I_{BQ} = \dfrac{V_{CC} - V_{BE}}{R_B} = \dfrac{12V - 0.7V}{240k\Omega} = 47.08\mu A$

$I_{CQ} = \beta I_{BQ} = 50(47.08\mu A) = 2.35mA$

b. $V_{CEQ} = V_{CC} - I_C R_C = 12V - (2.35mA)(2.2k\Omega) = 6.83V$

c. $V_B = V_{BE} = 0.7V \quad V_C = V_{CE} = 6.83V$

d. $V_{BC} = V_B - V_C = 0.7V - 6.83V = -6.13V$

2.8 a. $I_B = \dfrac{V_{CC}-V_{BE}}{R_B+(1+\beta)R_E} = \dfrac{20\text{V}-0.7\text{V}}{430\text{k}\Omega+(51)\cdot(1\text{k}\Omega)} = \dfrac{19.3\text{k}\Omega}{481\text{k}\Omega} = 40.1\,\mu\text{A}$

b. $I_C = \beta I_B = (50)(40.1\,\mu\text{A}) \approx 2.01\text{mA}$

c. $V_{CE} = V_{CC}-I_C(R_C+R_E) = 20\text{V}-(2.01\text{mA})(2\text{k}\Omega+1\text{k}\Omega)$
$= 20\text{V}-6.03\text{V} = 13.97\text{V}$

d. $V_C = V_{CC}-I_C R_C = 20\text{V}-(2.01\text{mA})(2\text{k}\Omega) = 20\text{V}-4.02\text{V} = 15.98\text{V}$

e. $V_E = V_C-V_{CE} = 15.98\text{V}-13.97\text{V} = 2.01\text{V}$

f. $V_B = V_{BE}+V_E = 0.7\text{V}+2.01\text{V} = 2.71\text{V}$

g. $V_{BC} = V_B-V_C = 2.71\text{V}-15.98\text{V} = -13.27\text{V}$ (reverse-biased as required)

2.9 (a) We assume $I_1 \gg I_B$, so

$V_B \approx \dfrac{R_2}{R_1+R_2}V_{CC} = \dfrac{2.5}{2.5+6.5}\times 5\text{V} \approx 1.4\text{V}$

$I_{EQ} = \dfrac{V_E}{R_E} = \dfrac{V_B-V_{BEQ}}{R_E} = \dfrac{1.4-0.7}{450}\text{A} \approx 1.5\text{mA}$

$I_{CQ} \approx I_{EQ} = 1.5\text{mA}$

$I_{BQ} = \dfrac{I_{CQ}}{\beta} = \dfrac{1.5}{100} = 15\,\mu\text{A}$

$V_{CEQ} = V_{CC}-I_{CQ}(R_C+R_E) = 5\text{V}-1.5\times(0.5+0.45)\text{V} \approx 3.6\text{V}$

(b) Equivalent circuits:

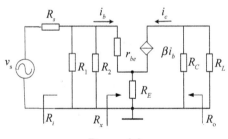

Figure p2.9

$v_o = -i_c(R_C/\!/R_L) = -\beta i_b(R_C/\!/R_L)$

$v_b = r_{be}+i_e R_E = i_b[r_{be}+(1+\beta)R_E]$

$r_{be} = 200+(1+\beta)\dfrac{26}{I_E} = 200+\dfrac{26}{I_B} = 200+\dfrac{26}{0.015} = 1.9\text{k}\Omega$

$$A_V = -\beta \frac{R_C /\!/ R_L}{r_{be} + (1+\beta)R_E} = -100 \frac{0.5 /\!/ 5}{1.9 + 101 \times 0.45} = -4.6$$

$R_x = v_b/i_b = r_{be} + (1+\beta)R_E = 47.35\text{k}\Omega$

$R_i = v_b/i_S = R_1 /\!/ R_2 /\!/ R_x = 6.5 /\!/ 2.5 /\!/ 47.35\text{k}\Omega$

$R_o = R_C = 500\Omega$

2.10

a. $I_B = \dfrac{V_{CC} - V_{BE}}{R_B + (\beta+1)R_E} = \dfrac{12\text{V} - 0.7\text{V}}{220\text{k}\Omega + (101)3.3\text{k}\Omega} = 20.42\mu\text{A}$

$I_E = (\beta+1)I_B = (101)(20.42\mu\text{A}) = 2.062\text{mA}$

$r_e = \dfrac{26\text{mV}}{I_E} = \dfrac{26\text{mV}}{2.062\text{mA}} = 12.61\text{k}\Omega$

b. $Z_b = \beta r_e + (\beta+1)R_E = (100)(12.61\Omega) + (101)(3.3\text{k}\Omega)$

$= 1.261\text{k}\Omega + 333.3\text{k}\Omega = 334.56\text{k}\Omega \cong \beta R_E$

$Z_i = R_B /\!/ Z_B = 220\text{k}\Omega /\!/ 334.56\text{k}\Omega = 132.72\text{k}\Omega$

$Z_o = R_E /\!/ r_e = 3.3\text{k}\Omega /\!/ 12.61\text{k}\Omega = 12.56\text{k}\Omega \cong r_e$

c. $A_V = \dfrac{V_o}{V_i} = \dfrac{R_E}{R_E + r_e} = \dfrac{3.3\text{k}\Omega}{3.3\text{k}\Omega + 12.61\text{k}\Omega} = 0.996 \cong 1$

2.11 $A_v = A_{v1}A_{v2} \approx -\dfrac{\beta_1 R'_{L1}}{r_{be1}} \times 1$, inside $R'_{L1} = R_{c1} /\!/ [r_{be2} + (1+\beta_2)(R_{e2} /\!/ R_L)]$

$R_i = r_{be1} /\!/ R_{b1} /\!/ R_{b2}$

$R_o = R_{e2} /\!/ \dfrac{R_{c1} + r_{be2}}{1+\beta_2}$

2.12 $I_E = \dfrac{V_{EE} - 0.7\text{V}}{R_E} = \dfrac{9\text{V} - 0.7\text{V}}{3.3\text{k}\Omega} \approx 2.5\text{mA}$

The collector current is then

$I_C = \dfrac{I_E}{2} = \dfrac{2.5\text{mA}}{2} = 1.25\text{mA}$

Resulting in a collector voltage of

$V_C = V_{CC} - I_C R_C = 9\text{V} - (1.25\text{mA})(3.9\text{k}\Omega) \approx 4.1\text{V}$

The common-emitter voltage is thus -0.7V, whereas the collector bias voltage is near 4.1V for both outputs.

2.13 (1) This circuit belong to common collector amplifier.

(2) $P_{OM} \approx \dfrac{1}{2}\dfrac{V_{CC}^2}{R_L} \Rightarrow V_{CC} = \sqrt{2P_{OM}R_L} = \sqrt{2\times 9\times 8}\,V = 12V$

(3) $P_{OM} = \dfrac{1}{2}\dfrac{(V_{CC}-V_{CES})^2}{R_L} = \dfrac{1}{2}\dfrac{(22-2)^2}{8}W = 22.5W$

2.14 (1) $P_o = \dfrac{V_o^2}{R_L} = \dfrac{10^2}{30} = 3.33W$,

$P_E = \dfrac{2V_{CC}V_{om}}{\pi R_L} = \dfrac{2\times 20\times 10\sqrt{2}}{\pi \times 30} = 6W$,

so $\eta = \dfrac{P_O}{P_E} = \dfrac{3.33}{6} = 55.5\%$

(2) $P_o = \dfrac{V_{om}^2}{2R_L} = \dfrac{20^2}{60} = 6.67W$,

$P_E = \dfrac{2V_{CC}V_{om}}{\pi R_L} = \dfrac{2\times 20\times 20}{\pi 30} = 8.49W$,

$\eta = \dfrac{P_O}{P_E} = 78.5\%$.

2.15 (1) D1 and D2 in the circuit minimized or eliminated the crossover distortion

(2) In static state, $U_{EQ} = 0V$;

(3) $P_{OM} = \dfrac{1}{2}\dfrac{(V_{CC}-V_{CES})^2}{R_L} = \dfrac{1}{2}\dfrac{(15-3)^2}{8}W = \dfrac{12^2}{16} = 9W$

$P_E = \dfrac{2V_{CC}V_{OM}}{\pi R_L} = \dfrac{2V_{CC}(V_{CC}-V_{CES})}{\pi R_L}W = \dfrac{2\times 15\times (15-3)^2}{\pi \times 8} = 13.2W$

$\eta = \dfrac{P_O}{P_E} = 68.2\%$

Chapter 3

3.1 (a) Parallel-current feedback

(b) Parallel-voltage feedback

(c) Series-current feedback

3.2 (a) Parallel-voltage feedback

(b) Series-current feedback

(c) Series-voltage feedback
(d) Series-current feedback
(e) Parallel-voltage feedback
(f) Series-voltage feedback

3.3 Using Equation $\left|\dfrac{dA_f}{A_f}\right| \cong \left|\dfrac{1}{FA}\right|\left|\dfrac{dA}{A}\right|$, we get

$$\left|\dfrac{dA_f}{A_f}\right| = \left|\dfrac{1}{-0.1(-1000)}(20\%)\right| = 0.2\%$$

The improvement is 100 times. Thus, wheres the amplifier gain changes from $|A|=1000$ by 20%, the gain with feedback from $|A_f|=100$ by only 0.2%.

3.4 $A_f = \dfrac{A}{1+AF} = \dfrac{-2000}{1+\left(-\dfrac{1}{10}\right)(-2000)} = -9.95$

Note that since $AF \gg 1$, $A_f \cong \dfrac{1}{F} = -10$

Chapter 4

4.1 The two conditions must be satisfied to sustain oscillation:
(1) The total phase shift must be $N \times 360°$, where $N = 10, 1, 2, \ldots$
    So, $-180° + 0° + 45° + \theta = N \times 360°$ $\theta = N \times 360° + 135°$
(2) The magnitude of the loop gain must be unity.
    So, $20 \times 0.01 \times A \times 0.7 = 1$ $A = 7.14$

4.2 An ideal op-amp is available and standard-valued resistors and capacitors are to be used.

$$RC = \dfrac{1}{2\pi f_0} = \dfrac{1}{2\pi(5 \times 10^3)} = 3.2 \times 10^{-5}$$

A 10kΩ resistor and 3.2 nF capacitor satisfy this requirement.

4.3 For the Colpitts oscillator, the oscillation frequency is

$$f_0 = \dfrac{1}{2\pi\sqrt{L\dfrac{C_1 C_2}{C_1 + C_2}}} = 500 \times 10^3$$

4.4 For the Hartley oscillator, the oscillation frequency is

$$f_0 = \dfrac{1}{2\pi\sqrt{(L_1 + L_2)C}} = 500 \times 10^3$$

You can choose inductance and capacitance to satisfy this requirement.

Chapter 5

5.1 (a) Non-inverting amplifier, use the gain equation solve directly,
$$v_o = \left(1 + \frac{33k}{33k}\right)v_i = 2 \times 0.1V = 0.2V$$

(b) Voltage follower, use the gain equation solve directly,
$$v_o = v_i = 1V$$

(c) The use of "virtual short", "false break" concept:
$$v_P = v_N, i_P = i_N = 0;$$
$$v_o = 1mA \times 10k\Omega = 10V$$

(d) The use of "virtual short", "false break" concept:
$$v_P = v_N, i_P = i_N = 0;$$
$$v_{P2} = v_i = 1V;$$
$$v_{N2} = v_{P2} = 1V;$$
$$v_o = v_{P1} = v_{N1} = \frac{1k + 0.5k}{1k} \times v_{N2} = 1.5V$$

5.2 $v_{o1} = \frac{10k + 110k}{10k} \cdot \frac{30k}{30k + 15k} = 8v_i$,

$v_o = v_{o1} = 8v_i = 800\sin\omega t$.

5.3 (1) S1 and S3 are closed, S2 is turned off, constitutes an inverting amplifier, $v_o = -v_i$.

(2) S1 and S2 is closed, S3 is turned off, $v_{P1} = v_{N1} = v_i, i = 0, v_o = v_i$.

(3) S2 is closed, the S1 and S3 are turned off, constitute non-inverting amplifier. $v_{P1} = v_{N1} = v_i, v_o = v_i$.

(4) S1, S2, S3 are closed when constituting an inverting amplifier, $v_o = -v_i$.

5.4 (1) The feedback resistor is R2, operational amplifier constitute inverting amplifier.
$$v_o = -\frac{R_2}{R_1}v_i = -\frac{200k}{100k} \times 2V = -4V$$

(2) The feedback resistor is $R_2 + \frac{RP}{2}$,
$$v_o = -\frac{R_2 + RP}{R_1}v_i = -\frac{200k + 2.5k}{100k} \times 2V = -4.05V$$

(3) The operational amplifier constitute voltage comparator. Add $V_i = 2V$ to the op amp's inverting terminal while non-inverting terminal is applied 0V. Voltage comparator output $v_o = -15V$.

5.5 $V_{o1} = -\dfrac{100k}{20k} \times v_i = -\dfrac{100k}{20k} \times 1V = -5V;$

$V_{o2} = -\dfrac{10k}{10k} \times V_{o1} = 5V;$

$V_o = V_{o2} - V_{o1} = 5V - (-5V) = 10V$

5.6 $v_{o1} = \left(1 + \dfrac{100k}{10k}\right) \times v_i = 11 \times 0.1V = 1.1V;$

$v_{o2} = -\dfrac{1}{RC}\int_0^t v_{o1}\,dt = -\dfrac{1}{100 \times 10^3 \times 10 \times 10^{-6}}\int_0^5 1.1\,dt$

$= 1.1 \times (5 - 0) = 5.5V$

5.7 Use inverting adder formula,

$$\dfrac{v_{i1}}{20k} + \dfrac{v_{i2}}{15k} + \dfrac{v_{i3}}{10k} = \dfrac{-v_o}{30k}$$

$$v_o = -(1.5v_{i1} + 2v_{i2} + 3v_{i3})$$

Substitute $v_o = 3V$, $v_{i1} = 1V$, $v_{i2} = -4.5V$, into the formula, can calculate $v_{i3} = 1.5V$. So send out warning signal when $v_{i3} = 1.5V$.

5.8 $v_o = \left(\dfrac{10k\Omega}{10k\Omega + 10k\Omega}\right)\left(\dfrac{150k\Omega + 300k\Omega}{150k\Omega}\right)v_1 - \dfrac{300k\Omega}{150k\Omega}v_2 = 0.5(3)(1V) - 2(2V) = 1.5V - 4V = -2.5V$

5.9 $f_{OH} = \dfrac{1}{2\pi R_1 C_1} = \dfrac{1}{2\pi(2.2k\Omega)(0.5\mu F)} = 1.45\text{kHz}$

5.10

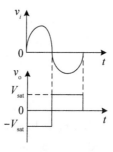

Figure p5.10

5.11 $V_d = V_{i1} - V_{i2} = (150 - 140)\mu V = 10\mu V$

$V_C = \frac{1}{2}(V_{i1} + V_{i2}) = \frac{150\mu V + 140\mu V}{2} = 145\mu V$

$V_o = A_d V_d \left(1 + \frac{1}{CMRR} \frac{V_c}{V_d}\right) = (4000)(10\mu V)\left(1 + \frac{1}{100} \frac{145\mu V}{10\mu V}\right)$

$= 40mV(1.145) = 45.8mV$

Chapter 6

6.1 (1)(b), (2)(d), (3)(c), (4)(c).

6.2 Digital representation has certain advantages over analog representation in electronics applications. For one thing, digital data can be processed and transmitted more efficiently and reliably than analog data. Also, digital data has a great advantage when storage is necessary. For example, music when converted to digital form can be stored more compactly and reproduced with greater accuracy and clarity than is possible when it is in analog form. Noise (unwanted voltage fluctuations) does not affect digital data nearly as much as it does analog signals.

6.3 (a) The period is measured from the edge of one pulse to the corresponding edge of the next pulse. In this case T is measured from leading edge to leading edge, as indicated. T equals 10ms.

(b) $f = \frac{1}{T} = \frac{1}{10ms} = 100Hz$

(c) Duty cycle $= \left(\frac{t_w}{T}\right) 100\% = \left(\frac{1ms}{10ms}\right) 100\% = 10\%$

Chapter 7

7.1 The whole number digit 5 has a weight of 100, which is 10^2, the digit 6 has a weight of 10, which is 10^1, the digit 8 has a weight of 1, which is 10^0, the fractional digit 2 has a weight of 0.1, which is 10^{-1}, and the fractional digit 3 has a weight of 0.01, which is 10^{-2}.

$568.23 = (5 \times 10^2) + (6 \times 10^1) + (8 \times 10^0) + (2 \times 10^{-1}) + (3 \times 10^{-2})$
$= (5 \times 100) + (6 \times 10) + (8 \times 1) + (2 \times 0.1) + (3 \times 0.01)$
$= 500 + 60 + 8 + 0.2 + 0.03$

7.2 Determine the weight of each bit that is a 1, and then find the sum of the weights to get the decimal number.

Weight: 2^6 2^5 2^4 2^3 2^2 2^1 2^0
Binary number: 1 1 0 1 1 0 1

$$1101101 = 2^6+2^5+2^4+2^3+2^2+2^1+2^0 = 64+32+8+4+1 = 109$$

7.3 Determine the weight of each bit that is a 1, and then sum the weights to get the decimal fraction.

Weight: 2^{-1} 2^{-2} 2^{-3} 2^{-4}
Binary number: 0.1 0 1 1

$$0.1011 = 2^{-1}+2^{-2}+2^{-3}+2^{-4} = 0.5+0.125+0.0625 = 0.6875$$

7.5 The equivalent decimal addition is also shown for reference.

(a)   11   3   (b) 100   4
    + 11   + 3   + 10   + 2
    ─────   ─────   ─────   ─────
     110   6   110   6

(c)   111   7   (d) 110   6
    + 11   + 3   + 100   + 4
    ─────   ─────   ─────   ─────
     1010   10   1010   10

7.6
(a)   11   3   (b)   11   3
    - 01   - 1   - 10   - 2
    ─────   ─────   ─────   ─────
     10   2   01   1

Chapter 8

8.1 (a)
8.2 (e)
8.3 When the inverter input is 1, the output is 0.
8.4

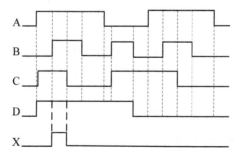

Figure p8.4

8.5

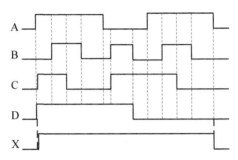

Figure p8.5

Chapter 9

9.1 (a) Let $A+B+C = X$ and $D = Y$. The expression $\overline{(A+B+C)D}$ is of the form $\overline{XY} = \overline{X} + \overline{Y}$ and can be rewritten as

$$\overline{(A+B+C)D} = \overline{A+B+C} + \overline{D}$$

Next, apply DeMorgan's thermo to term $\overline{(A+B+C)}$.

$$\overline{A+B+C} + \overline{D} = \overline{A}\overline{B}\overline{C} + D$$

(a) Let $ABC = X$ and $DEF = Y$. The expression $\overline{ABC + DEF}$ is of the form $\overline{X+Y} = \overline{X}\overline{Y}$ and can be rewritten as

$$(\overline{ABC})(\overline{DEF}) = (\overline{A}+\overline{B}+\overline{C})(\overline{D}+\overline{E}+\overline{F})$$

(C) Let $\overline{AB} = X$ and $\overline{CD} = Y$ and $EF = Z$. The expression $\overline{(\overline{AB}+\overline{CD}+EF)}$ is of the form $\overline{X+Y+Z} = \overline{X}\overline{Y}\overline{Z}$ and can be rewritten as

$$\overline{\overline{AB}+\overline{CD}+\overline{EF}} = (\overline{\overline{AB}})(\overline{\overline{CD}})(\overline{EF})$$

Next, Apply DeMorgan's theorem to each of the terms $\overline{\overline{AB}}, \overline{\overline{CD}}$ and $\overline{EF}$.

$$(\overline{\overline{AB}})(\overline{\overline{CD}})(\overline{EF}) = (\overline{A}+B)(C+\overline{D})(\overline{E}+\overline{F})$$

9.2 (a) $\overline{(A+B)} + C = (A+B)\overline{C}$

(b) $\overline{(\overline{A}+B)} + CD = \overline{(\overline{A}+B)}\,\overline{CD} = (\overline{\overline{AB}})(\overline{C}+\overline{D}) = A\overline{B}(\overline{C}+\overline{D})$

(c) $\overline{(A+B)\overline{CD}+E+\overline{F}} = \overline{((A+B)\overline{CD})(E+\overline{F})} = (\overline{AB}+C+D)\overline{E}F$

9.3 The following is not necessarity the only approach.

Step1. Apply the distributive law to the second and third terms in the expression, an follows:

$$AB+AB+AC+BB+BC$$

Step 2. Apply rule 7($BB=B$) to the fourth term.

$$AB+AB+AC+B+BC$$

Step 3. Apply rule 5($AB+AB=AB$) to the first two terms.

$$AB+AC+B+BC$$

Step 4. Apply rule 10($B+BC=B$) to the last two terms.

$$AB+AC+B$$

Step 5. Apply rule 10($AB+B=B$) to the first and third terms.

$$B+AC$$

9.4 Step1. Apply the distributive law to the law to the terms within the brackets.

$$(A\overline{B}C+A\overline{B}BD+\overline{AB})C$$

Step2. Apply rule 8($\overline{B}B=0$) to the second term within the parentheses.

$$(A\overline{B}C+A*0*D+\overline{AB})C$$

Step3. Apply rule 3($A*0*D=0$) to the second term within the parentheses.

$$(A\overline{B}C+0+\overline{AB})C$$

Step4. Apply rule 1(drop the 0) within the parentheses.

$$(A\overline{B}C+\overline{AB})C$$

Step5. Apply the distributive law.

$$A\overline{B}CC+\overline{AB}C$$

Step 6. Apply rule 7($CC=C$) to the first terms.

$$A\overline{B}C+\overline{AB}C$$

Step 7. Factor out $\overline{B}C$

$$\overline{B}C(A+\overline{A})$$

Step8. Apply rule 6($A+\overline{A}=1$)

$$\overline{B}C*1$$

Step9. Apply rule 4(drop the 1)

$$\overline{B}C$$

9.5 There are for 1s in the output column and the corresponding binary values are 011, 100, 110 and 111. These binary values are converted to product terms as follows:

$$011 \rightarrow \bar{A}BC$$
$$100 \rightarrow A\bar{B}\bar{C}$$
$$110 \rightarrow AB\bar{C}$$
$$111 \rightarrow ABC$$

The resulting standard SOP expression for the output X is

$$X = \bar{A}BC + A\bar{B}\bar{C} + AB\bar{C} + ABC$$

For the POS expression, the output is 0 for binary values 000, 001, 010, and 101. These binary values are converted to sum terms as follows:

$$000 \rightarrow A+B+C$$
$$001 \rightarrow A+B+\bar{C}$$
$$010 \rightarrow A+\bar{B}+C$$
$$101 \rightarrow \bar{A}+B+\bar{C}$$

The resulting standard POS expression for the output X is

$$X = (A+B+C)(A+B+\bar{C})(A+\bar{B}+C)(\bar{A}+B+\bar{C})$$

9.7 The SOP expression is obviously not in standard form because each product term does not have four variables. The first and second terms are both missing two variables, the third term is missing one variable, and the rest of the terms are standard. First, expand the terms by including all combinations of the missing variables numerically as follows:

$\bar{B}\bar{C}$	+	$A\bar{B}$	+	$AB\bar{C}$	+	$A\bar{B}C\bar{D}$	+	$\bar{A}\bar{B}CD$	+	$A\bar{B}CD$
0000		1000		1100		1010		0001		1011
0001		1001		1101						
1000		1010								
1001		1011								

Each of the resulting binary values is mapped by placing a 1 in the appropriate cell of the 4-variable Karnaugh map in Figure 4. Notice that some of the values in the expanded expression are redundant.

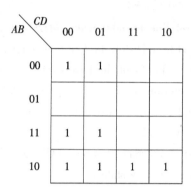

Figure p9.7

9.8 In the Figure 4.18, the product term for the 8-cell group is B because the cells within that group contain both A and $\bar{A}$, C and $\bar{C}$, D and $\bar{D}$, so these variables are eliminated. The 4-cell group contain $B, \bar{B}$, D and D, leaving the variables $\bar{A}$ and C, which form the product term $\bar{A}C$. The 2-cell group contains B and $\bar{B}$, leaving variables A, $\bar{C}$, and D which form the product term $A\bar{C}D$. Notice how overlapping is used to maximize the size of the groups. The resulting minimum SOP expression is the sum of these product terms:

$$B + \bar{A}C + A\bar{C}D$$

For the Karnaugh map in Figure p9.8, add a 1 in the lower right cell (1010) and determine the resulting SOP expression.

Chapter 10

10.1 (a) The input bits are $A = 1, B = 0$, and $C_{in} = 0$.

$1 + 0 + 0 = 1$ with no carry

Therefore, $\sum = 1$ and $C_{out} = 0$.

(b) The input bits are $A = 1, B = 1$, and $C_{in} = 0$.

$1 + 1 + 0 = 0$ with a carry of 1

Therefore, $\sum = 0$ and $C_{out} = 1$.

(c) The input bits are $A = 1, B = 0$, and $C_{in} = 1$.

$1 + 0 + 1 = 0$ with a carry of 1

Therefore, $\sum = 0$ and $C_{out} = 1$.

10.2 A 16-line-to-4 line encoder using 74LS148s and external logic. The 74LS148 can be expanded to a 16-line-to-4 line encoder by connecting the EO of the higher-order encoder to the EI of the lower-order encoder and negative-ORing the corresponding binary outputs as shown in Figure p10.2. The EO is used as the fourth and most-significant bit. This particular configuration produces active-HIGH outputs for the 4-bit binary number.

10.4 The data output alternates between LOW and HIGH as the data-select inputs sequence through the binary states.

Chapter 11

11.1

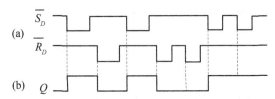

11.2 The Q waveform is shown in Figure. When S is HIGH and R is LOW, a HIGH on the EN input sets the latch. When S is LOW and R is HIGH, a HIGH on the EN input resets the latch. When both S and R are LOW, the Q output does not change from its present state.

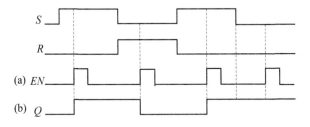

11.3 The Q output goes to the state of the D input at the time of the positive-going clock edge. The resulting output is shown in Figure.

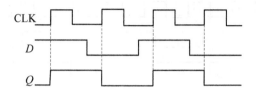

11.4 Since this is a negative edge-triggered flip-flop, as indicated by the "bubble" at the clock input, the Q output will change only on the negative-going edge of the clock pulse.

1. At the first clock pulse, both J and K are HIGH; and because this is a toggle condition, Q goes HIGH.

2. At clock pulse 2, a no-change condition exists on the inputs, keeping Q at a HIGH level.

3. When clock pulse 3 occurs, J is LOW and K is HIGH, resulting in a RESET condition; Q goes LOW.

4. At clock pulse 4, J is HIGH and K is LOW, resulting in a SET condition; Q goes HIGH.

5. A SET condition still exists on J and K when clock pulse 5 occurs, so Q will remain HIGH.

The resulting Q waveform is indicated in Figure p11.4.

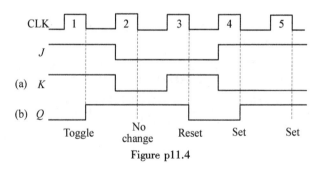

Figure p11.4

11.5 The Q output assumes the state determined by the states of the J and K inputs at the positive-going edge (triggering edge) of the clock pulse. A change in J or K after the triggering edge of the clock has no effect on the output, as shown in Figure p11.5.

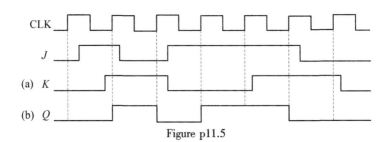

(a) K
(b) Q

Figure p11.5

11.6 The output timing diagram is shown in Figure p11.6. Notice that the outputs change on the negative-going edge of the clock pulses. The outputs go through the binary sequence 000, 001, 010, 011, 100, 101, 110, and 111 as indicated.

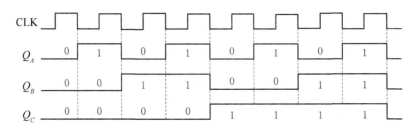

Figure p11.6

11.7 Use Equations:

$$f = \frac{1.44}{(R_1 + 2R_2)C_1} = \frac{1.44}{(2.2k\Omega + 9.4k\Omega)0.022\mu F} = 5.64 \text{kHz}$$

$$\text{Duty cycle} = \left(\frac{R_1 + R_2}{R_1 + 2R_2}\right)100\% = \left(\frac{2.2k\Omega + 4.7k\Omega}{2.2k\Omega + 9.4k\Omega}\right)100\% = 59.5\%$$

Chapter 12

12.1 (1) (a), (2) (b), (3) (b), (4) (c), (5) (c), (6) (c), (7) (b), (8) (d), (9) (b), (10) (c), (11) (a), (12) (c).

12.2 Initially, a bit pattern of 1000 (or any other pattern) can be synchronously preset into the counter by applying the bit pattern to the parallel data inputs, taking the SH/$\overline{\text{LD}}$ input LOW, and applying a clock pulse. After this initialization, the 1 continues to circulate through the ring counter, as the timing diagram in Figure p12.2 shows.

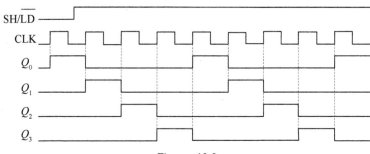

Figure p12.2